DATA VISUALIZATION
FOR BUSINESS DECISIONS

LICENSE, DISCLAIMER OF LIABILITY, AND LIMITED WARRANTY

DATA VISUALIZATION FOR BUSINESS DECISIONS

A Laboratory Manual

Third Edition

Andres Fortino, PhD

MERCURY LEARNING AND INFORMATION

Dulles, Virginia
Boston, Massachusetts
New Delhi

Publisher: David Pallai
MERCURY LEARNING AND INFORMATION
22841 Quicksilver Drive
Dulles, VA 20166
info@merclearning.com
www.merclearning.com
1-800-232-0223

A. Fortino. *Data Visualization for Business Decisions: A Laboratory Manual 3/E.*
ISBN: 978-1-68392-595-8

The publisher recognizes and respects all marks used by companies, manufacturers, and developers as a means to distinguish their products. All brand names and product names mentioned in this book are trademarks or service marks of their respective companies. Any omission or misuse (of any kind) of service marks or trademarks, etc. is not an attempt to infringe on the property of others.

Library of Congress Control Number: 2020939909

202122321   Printed on acid-free paper in the United States of America.

Our titles are available for adoption, license, or bulk purchase by institutions, corporations, etc. For additional information, please contact the Customer Service Dept. at 800-232-0223(toll free).

All of our titles are available for sale in digital format at *academiccourseware.com* and other digital vendors. Companion files for this title can also be downloaded by writing to *info@ merclearning.com*. The sole obligation of MERCURY LEARNING AND INFORMATION to the purchaser is to replace the book, based on defective materials or faulty workmanship, but not based on the operation or functionality of the product.

In gratitude to the art teachers of my youth,
Maestro Viera and Mrs. Greene.
Their lessons were inspirational and indelible.

Contents

Preface

This workbook is written for business analysts who wish to increase their skills in improving data visuals and creating compelling presentations used to support business decisions. It is a qualitative lab to develop the power of visualization and discrimination. It does not require the reader to modify charts but to analyze and describe what would improve those charts. In a set of guided exercises, the reader is taken through the eighteen elements of the six dimensions of analyzing and improving charts and visuals used to communicate business points.

An analyst, or anyone analyzing data, would typically create visuals of the analysis results as the analysis goes along. These are graphs of data for analysis; they are rough with no thought given to making them compelling at the point of analysis. Probably no one other than the analyst will ever see those rough analysis charts. These graphs may even accumulate in an electronic research notebook (typically a PowerPoint document) with slides as containers for the analysis charts. At the end of the analysis, these graphs and numerical summaries of results are used to draw conclusions and answer questions.

Then comes time to communicate. Often, analysts are not given a lot of time to present their findings. This is where the work of neurobiologist John Medina comes in to play. He advises us to use no more than ten minutes to make our case, lest we bore our audience to inattention. In any event, we must present our findings with as few slides as possible. The analyst looks over the rough graphs produced in analysis, looks at the conclusions, and then asks: "which of these are the most powerful visuals to make the point and underscore conclusions most compellingly?" There are probably no more than three or four such visuals that have to be created. Not created because they are there from the analysis, but recreated or enhanced, to make them more readable to new eyes.

The next step is to create those compelling visuals that tell the story. That's what these exercises help you do: refine your skills in turning a rough graph into a compelling visual. One way to do that is to refine your "seeing eye." Can you see what is wrong with a rough chart? What must be done to make it better? How do you improve a chart to make it more compelling? Many issues are very subtle, so it takes work to develop a trained sense of sight. Do the exercises in this book often, and the process will become second nature. As you work through these exercises, you will internalize the observe-analyze-refine process to improve your visuals.

On the Companion Files

The exercises require the analyst to have access to the case study slides and the analysis worksheet template, both of which are contained on the companion disc. These files, as well as video tutorials, for each chapter are also available for download from the publisher by writing to info@merclearning.com. As you learn about the principles explained in the book, you will be prompted to analyze charts created for a business purpose: the promotion of raising the US minimum wage by a government entity. Each principle presented in each of the chapters has a short companion video you may use to understand the ideas further. The video lessons may be found on the disc or by writing to the publisher. If you wish to stream the video rather than download it, there is a document in the companion files with links to all the companion videos to be found on a streaming service. The companion files also include a copy of the slides set used in the exercises and a copy of the analysis checklist used in the book.

Dr. Andres Fortino
June 2020

CHAPTER 1

THE LABS

The Lab Exercises

There are eighteen labs, three for each of the six major dimensions of analysis of data visuals in this class. The task for each exercise in the labs is to consider charts from a public presentation created by a US government agency. We evaluate charts using a checklist of the dimensions covered in class looking for what works and does not work. Depending on the results of your analysis, you are then asked to consider what you would do to improve the chart to better align it with each dimension.

We do this for one of the charts in the document and provide an expert opinion solution to compare to your analysis. The opinion is supported by the reasons why the chart was scored that way, as well as opinion on what can be done to improve it. The reader is then guided to analyzing and improving a second chart from the document as additional practice.

The source of the charts is a public historical document provided by the US Government Council of Economic Advisors promoting policy changes to the minimum wage across the United States. The details of this case study and how to use it are discussed in the section entitled The Case Study.

At the end of all labs, there is a final exercise to review the aggregate analysis and final results for the two charts analyzed and provide an overview road map to improve any chart.

The Six Dimensions

We analyze the chart in six dimensions with three aspects each, making a total of eighteen directions of analysis:

Story Dimension	Purpose Dimension	Method Dimension
Visual Story	Need	Color
Visual Props	Audience	Chart Junk
Storytellers	Frame	Title

Sign Dimension	**Perception Dimension**	**Chart Dimension**
Sign	Seeing	Right Chart
Communication	Mind	Selection
Function	Quality	Tables

The Exercises

The six labs will help you practice analyzing charts along these six dimensions, with each lab containing six exercises. There are two well-worked-out exercises for each of the eighteen directions of analysis. Make sure to use the analysis template in this lab book. Fill it out as you go along.

Go through Part A of each exercise in the lab and check yourself against the expert's opinion. Pay particular attention to where you and the expert disagree. Look at why the expert selected the answer they did and their rationale. Also, try to improve the chart along these dimensions. Again, check yourself against the expert's opinion.

You can reinforce your skills by doing Part B of each exercise based on a second chart, as outlined in the workbook. Once you have completed that, select any other chart in the case study set (see the end of the lab manual for more charts) and repeat for more practice.

Internalizing the Process

Although practitioners wishing to improve their skills in improving charts can continue to use the analysis template after they have completed the labs, this is not the envisioned continued use of the checklist. We propose that you use the analysis template for these labs and get familiar with how to use it, and with the process. Then use it a few more times on actual charts in your everyday work.

Eventually, repeated use of this process and the checklist will result in the internalization of the analysis, and you will no longer need the checklist. Essentially, you are training your eye and your perception to see charts in more and more detail over time. In time you will acquire new strategies to correct anything that seems to need improvement in charts. You will find that you will be asking the questions in the analysis template naturally, answering them, and improving your charts accordingly.

As you use these exercises, you will see your chart-making skills go to the next level.

CHAPTER 2

THE CASE STUDY

The Case Study

The case study is based on a set of slides posted by the executive branch of the United States government, used to promote a certain policy initiative. Early in President Obama's administration, there was a push to have all states in the union, as well as the federal government, adopt a higher minimum wage level than was prevalent at that time. One of the agencies of the executive branch is the Council of Economic Advisors. They laid out the economic case for raising the minimum wage. This slide set was made available at the time via the White House website to educate the public, policymakers, and lawmakers. We want to see if we can improve the charts in the presentation, which was the chosen communication platform.

Your Task

Read the entire document (it consists mostly of slides, so it's easy). You will find the material at the end of this lab book. From your reading, you should get a sense of why the document was written. You should also try to discover who the audience is, what the authors are trying to say, and what the authors are trying to accomplish. You should ask these questions: Are the authors trying to inform? To get the audience to take action? What action? To move the audience to support a policy with their representatives? Who are the members of the audience? Who are the authors? What is their profession? Are they authority figures? What are their credentials?

Forming some idea of the answers to these questions informs your understanding of the charts and what they are meant to accomplish. You may be doing a lot of conjecture. That's understandable and, without better knowledge, we will take that as our starting point of analysis. It's from that point of view you will be critiquing and improving the charts.

Think of yourself as a staff member of the Council of Economic Advisors, the group that created this presentation. One day you are called into the office of the chief economist, and he (or she) says: "Since you are one of our best data visualization experts on staff, I would like you to look over this document and tell us how we can improve these charts. We want to have the greatest impact on our readers." That's the basis of our analysis.

We will analyze some of the charts to see if they can be improved. For that purpose, we will use the scoring tool provided in this lab manual. For each lab, we will accumulate the score for each of the six dimensions in the tool until, after we have finished the last lab, we will have a complete picture of how effective the chart is (or is not). More importantly, when we analyze each of the three dimensions in each lab, we will consider what can be done to improve the chart.

This exercise is intended to refine your power of discrimination so you can spot the flaws in a visual and do something about it.

NOTE *You may reinforce these principles by watching the video tutorials on these topics found in the companion files on the disc or by downloading them from the publisher by writing to info@merclearning.com.*

CHAPTER 3

THE ANALYSIS TOOL

An Analysis Tool for Visuals

We will use the analysis template provided with this manual to analyze and improve a chart or data visualization along the six dimensions outlined previously and discussed in detail at the start of each lab. We are not trying to get the analysis perfect or use the template with a great degree of accuracy. It is a tool to guide the eye and your discrimination. Using the analysis template and the associated questions produces an imperfect indicator, and it should be sufficient to guide you in making improvements to any chart. We hope that by using the tool multiple times, you will then begin to internalize the questions and, eventually, you will not need to use the tool.

To use the tool, consider answering the question associated with each principle. Consider each question and then use the following rough criteria: answer YES if the chart fulfills the question for the most part (>70%), and NO if the chart is deficient in that question (<70%). This process requires a rough pass-fail judgment on the issue. It's not perfect, and it is not meant to create an exact measurement of the visual's perfection. It is meant to develop and refine your power of discrimination when analyzing and improving charts: what looks good, what does not.

The next few pages provide a copy of the analysis template to print as a reference. You can copy it and use paper and pencil if you wish. Or use it electronically by using your favorite editor. Use a different template for each chart being analyzed. You can use the template as provided right in this book.

NOTE *This template, all of the files for the text, as well as video tutorials for each exercise are available on the companion disc or for downloading by writing to the publisher at info@merclearning.com*

Data Visualization for Business Decisions: Analyzing a Visual Analysis Template

Story

Visual Story – A picture is worth a thousand words

- *Is the point of the visual very clear?*

Visual Props – Visuals support the story; they are not the story.

- *Has the visual has been simplified and focused?*

Storytellers – Standing on the shoulder of giants

- *Are past masters and the basic charts that they pioneered emulated?*

Analysis of Story

- *What is wrong with the visual being analyzed along this dimension?*
- *What can be done to improve the visual along this dimension?*

Signs

Signs – Bertin: Semiotics, signs, and signifiers

- *Is the use of signs and symbols appropriate?*

Communication – Visualization as a communication system

- *Is the Signal-to-Noise ratio high?*

Function – Cairo: The Functional Art – Art vs. Clarity

- *Is the chart functionally informational rather than beautiful art?*

Analysis of Signs

- *What is wrong with the visual being analyzed along this dimension?*
- *What can be done to improve the visual along this dimension?*

Purpose

Need – Needs of the requester and the organization

- *Does the chart fulfill organizational information needs?*

Audience – Cairo: Audience needs, biases, and journey

- *Does the chart allow for audience biases, needs, and journeys?*

Frame – Shron: Thinking with Data CoNVO model

- *Does the visual answer a well-framed analytical question?*

Analysis of Purpose

- *What is wrong with the visual being analyzed along this dimension?*
- *What can be done to improve the visual along this dimension?*

Perception

Seeing – Anatomy: the human eye-brain system

- *Does the eye of the viewer focus on the most important point being made?*

Mind – Gestalt: the psychology of perception

- *Have the principles of the Gestalt psychology of perception been thoughtfully employed in the visual?*

Quality – Alexander: Quality without a Name

- *Does the visual inform the viewer and dispel his ignorance?*

Analysis of Perception

- *What is wrong with the visual being analyzed along this dimension?*
- *What can be done to improve the visual along this dimension?*

Method

Color – Use of color, dysfunctions

- *Is color used judiciously and sparsely?*

Chart Junk – Tufte: Chart junk

- *Is the visual clear of unnecessary visual elements not leading to a clear point being made?*

Title – McKinsey: A Better Way to Title Charts

- *Does the title of the chart convey the point being made with the chart?*

Analysis of Method

- *What is wrong with the visual being analyzed along this dimension?*
- *What can be done to improve the visual along this dimension?*

Charts

Right Chart – Cleveland and McGill: Functional Scale

- Does the type of chart being used match the level of judgment required?

Selection – The Basic Charts

- Does the chart type used match the business question being answered?

Tables – Analyze or Tell?

- Are referenceable visuals (tables) readable with appropriate conditional formatting and thumbnail graphs used for emphasis?

Analysis of Charts

- What is wrong with the visual being analyzed along this dimension?
- What can be done to improve the visual along this dimension?

CHAPTER 4

STORY

Visual Story Telling

As one visual storyteller, Al Shallowly, tells it, visualizations are like the old campfire around which we used to gather to tell each other stories. Are we telling compelling business stories with our visuals?

Create a Visual Story

As the saying goes, a picture is worth a thousand words. Does your visual make a clear point that would take a lot of words to convey? What is the point of the visual? Does your audience get the point? Is your story clear?

Rather than use 1,000 words to describe the point of your data—show it! We will assume that you are working on business issues. You have data that point to the direction managers should take on the issues and support certain actions. Rather than describe the facts in words, draw a picture—not just by presenting the data. Do not "Let the data speak for itself," but rather "Tell your story." Draw a picture. The point of the visual is to make a business point. The data-driven visual has to convey the point unambiguously.

Usually, use one point per visual, or several, if in a dashboard. The point we are trying to make is a business point. It must be tied to business metrics. It is most effective when tied to fundamental metrics like KPIs (Key Performance Indicators) and CSFs (Critical Success Factors) that have been adopted by the organization. Visuals are always most effective when dealing with fundamental financial implications.

> *The point of this principle is that for a data visualization to be most successful, your visual should make the business point very clear—that is the story you are telling.*

Make It a Prop

Famous chart maker Stephen Few admonishes us that numbers have an important story to tell. Our numbers rely on us to give them a compelling voice.

A data visual should not tell the whole story but be a prop to be used by the storyteller. Charts support the storyteller. Charts are not the whole story. Charts are a complement for the storyteller by summarizing complex data in a single image.

A picture as a prop has few words. The story (making the argument) is delivered orally or in written prose by the storyteller, the presenter. The data visual in that case should be streamlined to deliver complex data analysis conclusions succinctly to support the presenter, the presentation, the written prose, and the oral arguments, not supplant the presenter.

The visual supports the story.

Analysis often produces many views of the data, many graphs. We don't bring them all to a presentation. Out of the many select a few that best support the conclusions of the analysis—that's the story you bring to the audience. These select few graphs have to be compelling. They have to be polished.

> *The point of this principle is that for a data visualization to be most successful, the data visual used to support a presentation should be a prop and not be self-contained*

Emulate Legendary Storytellers

We have a rich data visualization heritage; we stand on the shoulder of giants, as it were.

They are master storytellers who invented and used data visuals as their props. The question is, can you improve your visual by emulating famous chart makers? Are your visuals rooted in their iconic chart exemplars?

For example, see the work of folks like John Snow with his London Cholera Map; Charles Minard and Napoleon's March on Moscow; Hans Rosling, who invented Gapminder and moving bubble diagrams; Joseph Priestley and his Chart of Biography and his New Chart of History; and finally, Florence Nightingale and her radar charts of the Crimean War.

> *The point of this principle is that for a data visualization to be most successful, we should study and learn how past visualization masters employed the basic charts that they pioneered.*

The Exercises

The next three exercises in this lab help you practice analyzing charts along these three dimensions. There are two well-worked-out exercises. Make sure to use the analysis template. Fill it out as you go along. In the end, after you have gone through the eighteen exercises, you can see what the aggregate scores are in the summary tab.

Go through each exercise in the section and check yourself against the expert's opinion. Pay particular attention to where you and the expert disagree. Look at why the expert selected their answer and their rationale. Also, try to improve the chart along these dimensions. Again, check yourself against the expert's opinion.

You can reinforce your skills by doing each exercise for the second chart, as outlined in the manual. Once you are done with that, select any other chart in the case study set (see the end of the lab manual for more charts).

NOTE *As a reminder, all of the companion files and video tutorials for the exercises are available on the disc or for downloading by writing to the publisher at info@merclearning.com.*

Exercise 1: Creating Visual Stories

1. Consider the first chart (Figure 4.1) in the case study. Analyze it along the Story dimension.

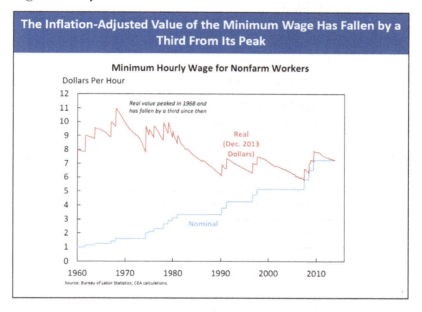

FIGURE 4.1 The Inflation-Adjusted Value of the Minimum Wage Has Fallen by a Third from Its Peak

2. Using the analysis checklist, answer each question for this principle. Remember that for a yes answer, you should feel more than 70% confident it's a YES. Otherwise, answer it as NO. The NO answers should give you indicators on what is wrong with this chart and what needs correction.

Visual Story – A picture is worth a thousand words

- Does the visual make a clear point that would take a lot of words to convey?

- Is the point of the visual clear?

- Does the viewer quickly get the point?

- Is the story clear?

- Does the visual support a business story, not a story of your analysis journey?

- Does the viewer understand the import of the point the visual is trying to make?

Is the point of the visual obvious?

3. Now, look at the aspects of this dimension that you scored as deficient (scored a NO). Based on the Story principles you learned, what can you do to improve the chart?

Expert Solution

An expert may score this chart along the Story dimension as:

Visual Story - A picture is worth a thousand words	Yes	No
Does the visual make a clear point that would take a lot of words to convey?	x	
Is the point of the visual clear?		x
Do I get the point easily?		x
Is the story clear?		x
Does the visual support a business story, not an analysis journey story?	x	
Do I understand the import of the point the visual is trying to make?		x
The point the visual is very clear		2
		33%

We will make a major assumption as the basis of our analysis: these charts were directed to government policymakers (staff of the executive and legislative branches, and state and municipal governments). We will take this chart as part of a story to convince policymakers of the importance of adopting higher minimum wage standards in the country through legislation and administrative action.

On that basis, the major points where the chart does not work is that although the title of the graph tells us the point of the graph, the picture is hard to decipher. The data is accurate and correct and is the right data to use and display, and the choice of chart is probably a good one, but it does not show the major drop in the effective buying power of the minimum wage over the years even as the amount of the minimum wage has risen.

We suggest you would fix this chart by doing the following: perhaps using trend lines to show the stark rise in the amount of the minimum wage while its buying power was dramatically decreasing. There must be a way to make that dramatic drop to be more evident. One gets lost in the meandering stepwise lines, accurate but not compelling.

4. As an additional exercise, consider the fourth chart (Figure 4.2) in the case study. Analyze it along the Story dimension.

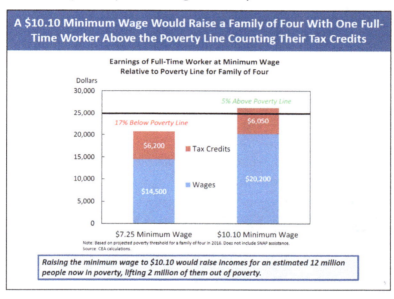

FIGURE 4.2 A $10.10 Minimum Wage Would Raise a Family of Four with One Full-Time Worker above the Poverty Line Counting Their Tax Credits

5. Using the analysis checklist, answer each question for this principle. Remember that for a yes answer, you should feel more than 70% confident for a YES. Otherwise, answer it as NO. The results should indicate what is wrong with this chart and what needs correction.

Visual Story – A picture is worth a thousand words

- Does the visual make a clear point that would take a lot of words to convey?

- Is the point of the visual clear?

- Does the viewer easily get the point?
- Is the story clear?
- Does the visual support a business story, not a story of your analysis journey?
- Does the viewer understand the import of the point the visual is trying to make?

Is the point of the visual very clear?

6. Now, look at the aspects of this dimension that you scored as deficient (those scored as NO). Based on the Story principles you learned in the companion class, what can you do to improve the chart?

Exercise 2: Use as a Prop

1. Consider the first chart (Figure 4.3) in the case study. Analyze it along the Props dimension.

FIGURE 4.3 The Inflation-Adjusted Value of the Minimum Wage Has Fallen by a Third from Its Peak

2. Using the analysis checklist, answer each question for this principle. Remember that for a yes answer, you should feel more than 70% confident, and then it's a YES. Otherwise, answer it as a NO. The answers should give you indicators on what is wrong with this chart and what needs correction.

Visual Props – Visuals support the story, they are not the story

- Is the visual a prop for oral delivery of the story?

- Have the textual elements on the slide that tell a story been minimized?

- Is the graph more of a visual prop and less of an infographic?

- Have the infographic elements been minimized?

- Has the most important type of analysis graph been selected to support the business story?

Has the visual been simplified and focused?

3. Now, look at the aspects of this dimension that you scored as deficient (scored a NO). Based on the Props principles you learned in the companion class, what can you do to improve the chart?

Expert Solution

An expert may score this chart along the Props dimension as:

Visual Props - Visuals support the story, they are not the story	Yes	No
Is the visual a prop for oral delivery of the story?		x
Have the textual elements on the slide that tell a story been minimized?	x	
Is the graph more of a visual prop and less of an infographic?	x	
Have the infographic elements been minimized?	x	
Has the most important type of analysis graph been selected to support the business story?		x
The visual has been simplified and focused	3	
	60%	

We will assume that this set of slides is probably used by the Council of Economic Advisors to brief policymakers on the policy initiative supported by the White House at the time.

The major point appears to be that the Council of Economic Advisors is also using this set of slides as a briefing book on the issue. You can't have it both ways. If it is used as a briefing book, the charts may be more detailed as these are. If used as props for a presentation, they need to be more compelling and less technical.

We suggest you would fix this chart by doing the following: use these slides as a basis for a more compelling set of charts and select better chart types, especially for this particular chart, that make the point better.

4. As an additional exercise, consider the fourth chart (Figure 4.4) in the case study. Analyze it along the Prop dimension.

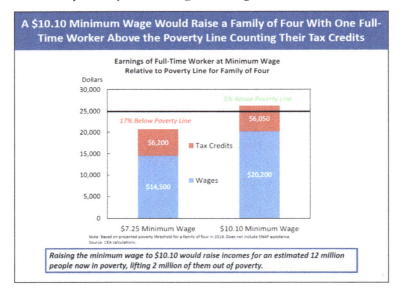

FIGURE 4.4 A $10.10 Minimum Wage Would Raise a Family of Four with One Full-Time Worker above the Poverty Line Counting Their Tax Credits

5. Using the analysis checklist, answer each question for this principle. Remember that for a yes answer, you should feel more than 70% confident, and then it's a YES. Otherwise, answer it as a NO. The answers should give you indicators on what is wrong with this chart and what needs correction.

Visual Props – Visuals support the story, they are not the story

- Is the visual a prop for oral delivery of the story?

- Have the textual elements on the slide that tell a story been minimized?

- Is the graph more of a visual prop and less of an infographic?

- Have the infographic elements been minimized?

- Has the most important type of analysis graph been selected to support the business story?

Has the visual been simplified and focused?

6. Now, look at the aspects of this dimension that you scored as deficient (scored a NO). Based on the Prop principles you learned in the companion class, what can you do to improve the chart?

Exercise 3: Emulating Storytellers

1. Consider the first chart (Figure 4.5) in the case study. Analyze it along the Storytellers dimension.

FIGURE 4.5 The Inflation-Adjusted Value of the Minimum Wage Has Fallen by a Third from Its Peak

2. Using the analysis checklist, answer each question for this principle. Remember that for a yes answer, you should feel more than 70% confident, and then it's a YES. Otherwise, answer it as a NO. The answers should give you indicators on what is wrong with this chart and what needs correction.

Storytellers – Standing on the shoulder of giants

- Is the visual improved by emulating famous chart makers?

- Does the visual have roots in an iconic master chart?

Are past masters and the basic charts that they pioneered emulated?

3. Now, look at the aspects of this dimension that you scored as deficient (scored a NO). Based on the Storytellers principles you learned in the companion class, what can you do to improve the chart?

Expert Solution

An expert may score this chart along the Storytellers dimension as:

Storytellers - Standing on the shoulder of giants	Yes	No
Is the visual improved by emulating famous chart makers?		x
Does the visual have roots in an iconic master chart?		x
Past masters and the basic charts that they pioneered are emulated	0	
	0%	

The major point is that there is probably a better, more compelling chart form, such as Playfair's iconic bar graphs.

We suggest you would fix this chart by changing to a bar chart, for example, that accentuates the upward flow of the minimum wage over the years versus the downward loss of its buying power.

4. As an additional exercise, consider the fourth chart (Figure 4.6) in the case study. Analyze it along the Storytellers dimension.

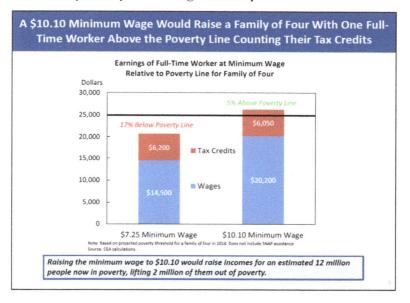

FIGURE 4.6 A $10.10 Minimum Wage Would Raise a Family of Four with One Full-Time Worker above the Poverty Line Counting Their Tax Credits

5. Using the analysis checklist, answer each question for this principle. Remember that for a yes answer, you should feel more than 70% confident, and then it's a YES. Otherwise, answer it as a NO. The answers should give you indicators on what is wrong with this chart and what needs correction.

Storytellers – Standing on the shoulder of giants

- Is the visual improved by emulating famous chart makers?

- Does the visual have roots in an iconic master chart?

Are past masters and the basic charts that they pioneered emulated?

6. Now, look at the aspects of this dimension that you scored as deficient (scored a NO). Based on the Storytellers principles you learned in the companion class, what can you do to improve the chart?

CHAPTER 5

SIGNS

Signs and Sign Making

Jacques Bertin explains in his *Semiology of Graphics* book that we transform data into graphs to increase our understanding. We interrogate maps and diagrams and charts, but we must integrate all of the data. We do that most efficiently by reducing it to a small number of elementary data elements.

We must become good sign makers and send strong, unmistakable signals to our audience of the direction they should take in their decision-making.

Give Them a Sign

People need a strong sign to be able to make good decisions. This is where Bertin's work on Semiotics (the art of sign making) comes in. Are we using signs and symbols properly in our visuals? Does the visual use cultural cues properly? Do we transgress any cultural conventions? Is our audience expecting the symbolism we use in our chart, or are they surprised and confused by it?

The science of sign making has three parts: (a) The signifier, the intended meaning; (b) The signified or significant, which is the symbol or icon that stands in for the signifier. For example, a "dog" is represented by a "picture of a dog"; and (c) The sign, the combination that makes up our understanding.

For a data visualization to be most successful, we must use signs and symbols appropriately.

It's Like a Communication System

Sign making for our charts is part of setting up a communication system. We must ask, as with any communication system, does our visual send a strong, unmistakable signal? Will the receiver, our audience, be able to decode it? Or is there too much noise, and what can we do to reduce it?

In an effective presentation, the audience gets your point even in the presence of noise. We encode our message, our story, in signs and symbols of a chart. We communicate it using a transmission system, slides in a presentation, a document, a video, a webcast. The receiver gets our transmission and decodes it: "what does it mean to me, to the numbers I have to make, to my team, to my company?" Were you clear, or did you let noise cloud making your point? Did you increase the signal over the noise?

> *For a data visualization to be most successful, we must encode our point clearly, so the audience decodes it meaningfully, so we must increase the Signal-to-Noise ratio.*

Design for Function

Our colleague and foremost data journalist Alberto Cairo, in his book *The Functional Art,* urges us to make our charts more functional than artistic. Our charts should inform not entertain.

We should ask ourselves as we create our charts: does the chart inform or entertain? We should avoid having our chart be prized and classified as beautiful art, especially if it fails to inform. We are talking about functionally over making the chart pretty. Avoid frilliness. Have we sacrificed clarity to make our chart pleasing to the eye? We should strive to inform, not to create a chart that appeals to emotions but rather to reason leading to good decisions.

> *For a data visualization to be most successful, make sure the chart is functionally informational rather than beautiful artwork.*

The Exercises

The next three exercises in this lab help you practice analyzing charts along these three dimensions. There are two well-worked-out exercises. Make sure to use the tool in the accompanying spreadsheet. Fill it out as you go along. In the end, after you have gone through the eighteen exercises, you can see what the aggregate scores are in the summary tab.

Go through each exercise in the section and check yourself against the expert's opinion. Pay particular attention to where you and the expert disagree. Look at why the expert selected the answer they did and their rationale. Also, try to improve the chart along these dimensions. Again, check yourself against the expert's opinion.

You can reinforce your skills by doing each exercise for a second chart, as outlined in the workbook. Once you are done with that exercise, select any other chart in the case study set (see the end of the lab manual for more charts) and repeat.

NOTE
You may reinforce these principles by watching the video tutorials on these topics found in the companion files on the disc or by downloading them from the publisher by writing to info@merclearning.com.

Exercise 4: Using Signs

1. Consider the first chart (Figure 5.1) in the case study. Analyze it along the Signs dimension.

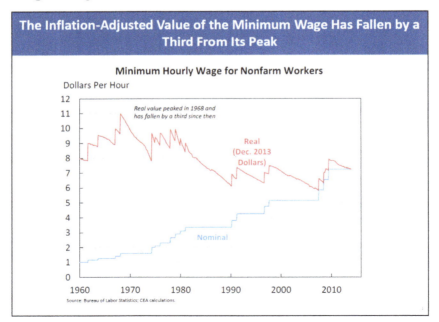

FIGURE 5.1 The Inflation-Adjusted Value of the Minimum Wage Has Fallen by a Third from Its Peak

2. Using the analysis checklist, answer each question for this principle. Remember that for a yes answer, you should feel more than 70% confident, and then it's a YES. Otherwise, answer it as a NO. The answers should give you indicators on what is wrong with this chart and what needs correction.

Signs – Bertin: Semiotics, signs, and signifiers

- Are signs and symbols used properly in the visual?

- Are cultural cues used properly in the visual?

- The visual does not transgress cultural conventions?

- Is the symbolism in the chart, and that represented by the chart, expected by the viewer?

Is the use of signs and symbols appropriate?

3. Now, look at the aspects of this dimension that you scored as deficient (scored a NO). Based on the Signs principles you learned in the companion class, what can you do to improve the chart?

Expert Solution

An expert may score this chart along the Signs dimension as:

Signs - Bertain: Semiotics, sign and signifiers	Yes	No
Are signs and symbols used properly in the visual?		x
Are cultural cues used properly in the visual?		x
The visual does not transgress cultural conventions?	x	
Is the symbolism in the chart, and that represented by the chart, expected by the viewer?		x
The use of signs and symbols is appropriate	**1**	
	25%	

The major point is that the designers of the chart did make a clear sign that the buying power of the minimum wage has been decreasing dramatically over the years, while seemingly the amount of the minimum wage has been increasing. The viewer has to study the chart for a while to infer this conclusion. Even though the title tells the story, the data does not easily support the message. No clear sign has been given. Again, probably the designers are speaking to economists, technical people who easily derive this knowledge from the chart given.

We suggest you would fix this chart by making the lowering of the buying power of wages over time more obvious.

4. As an additional exercise, consider the fourth chart (Figure 5.2) in the case study. Analyze it along the Signs dimension.

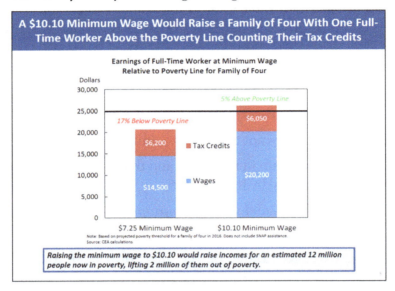

FIGURE 5.2 A $10.10 Minimum Wage Would Raise a Family of Four with One Full-Time Worker above the Poverty Line Counting Their Tax Credits

5. Using the analysis checklist, answer each question for this principle. Remember that for a yes answer, you should feel more than 70% confident, and then it's a YES. Otherwise, answer it as a NO. The answers should give you indicators on what is wrong with this chart and what needs correction.

Signs – Bertin: Semiotics, signs, and signifiers

- Are signs and symbols used properly in the visual?

- Are cultural cues used properly in the visual?

- Does the visual transgress cultural conventions?

- Is the symbolism in the chart, and that represented by the chart, expected by the viewer?

Is the use of signs and symbols appropriate?

6. Now, look at the aspects of this dimension that you scored as deficient (scored a NO). Based on the Signs principles you learned in the companion class, what can you do to improve the chart?

Exercise 5: Communications Systems

1. Consider the first chart (Figure 5.3) in the case study. Analyze it along the Communications dimension.

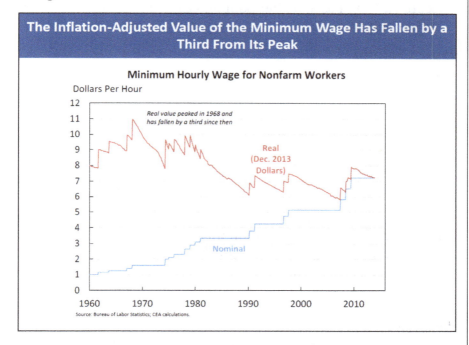

FIGURE 5.3 The Inflation-Adjusted Value of the Minimum Wage Has Fallen by a Third from Its Peak

2. Using the analysis checklist, answer each question for this principle. Remember that for a yes answer, you should feel more than 70% confident, and then it's a YES. Otherwise, answer it as a NO. The answers should give you indicators on what is wrong with this chart and what needs correction.

Communication – Visualization as a communication system

- Does the visual send a strong, unmistakable signal?
- Will the receiver be able to decode the signal?
- Is the noise minimized?

Is the Signal-to-Noise ratio high?

3. Now, look at the aspects of this dimension that you scored as deficient (scored a NO). Based on the Communications principles you learned in the companion class, what can you do to improve the chart?

Expert Solution

An expert may score this chart along the Communications dimension as:

Communication - Visualization as a communication system	Yes	No
Does the visual send a strong unmistakable signal?		x
Will the receiver be able to decode the signal?		x
Is the noise minimized?	x	
The Signal to Noise ratio is high		1
		33%

The major point is that the important signal is the dramatic decrease in the buying power of the minimum wage. We see that the minimum wage and its buying power are equal at the right of the chart, which could send a signal that all is well. It's not that bad, so what, buying power and minimum wage are equal. That's good, isn't it? What is dramatic is the ratio of the minimum wage to buying power. At the start of the chart it is 8:1 and at the end it is 1:1. It takes a while for the reader or viewer to come to this startling fact. That's the premise for making a case for a raise in the minimum wage, no? That signal is lost by presenting the data flat, not in a meaningful way.

Other than that, the chart is very clear, noise is minimized, and only one point is being made.

We could fix this chart by adding a trend line of the ratio of buying power to minimum wage.

4. As an additional exercise, consider the fourth chart (Figure 5.4) in the case study. Analyze it along the Communications dimension.

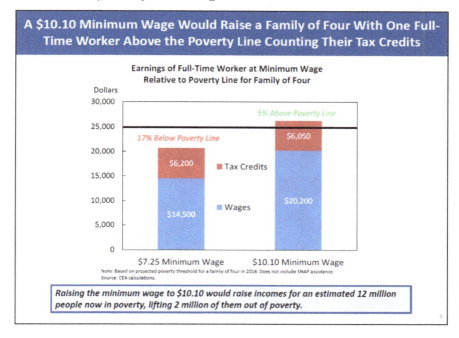

A $10.10 Minimum Wage Would Raise a Family of Four With One Full-Time Worker Above the Poverty Line Counting Their Tax Credits

Earnings of Full-Time Worker at Minimum Wage
Relative to Poverty Line for Family of Four

Dollars

5% Above Poverty Line

17% Below Poverty Line

$6,050

$6,200

■ Tax Credits

$20,200

■ Wages

$14,500

$7.25 Minimum Wage $10.10 Minimum Wage

Note: Based on projected poverty threshold for a family of four in 2016. Does not include SNAP assistance.
Source: CEA calculations.

Raising the minimum wage to $10.10 would raise incomes for an estimated 12 million people now in poverty, lifting 2 million of them out of poverty.

FIGURE 5.4 A $10.10 Minimum Wage Would Raise a Family of Four with One Full-Time Worker above the Poverty Line Counting Their Tax Credits

5. Using the analysis checklist, answer each question for this principle. Remember that for a yes answer, you should feel more than 70% confident, and then it's a YES. Otherwise, answer it as a NO. The answers should give you indicators on what is wrong with this chart and what needs correction.

Communication – Visualization as a communication system

- Does the visual send a strong, unmistakable signal?
- Will the receiver be able to decode the signal?
- Is the noise minimized?

Is the Signal-to-Noise ratio high?

6. Now, look at the aspects of this dimension that you scored as deficient (scored a NO). Based on the Communications principles you learned in the companion class, what can you do to improve the chart?

Exercise 6: Functional Design

1. Consider the first chart (Figure 5.5) in the case study. Analyze it along the Function dimension.

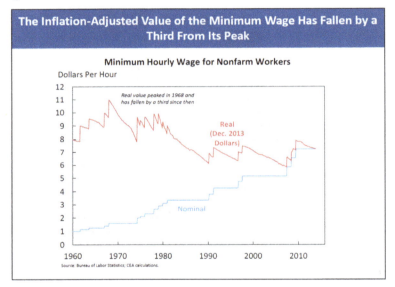

FIGURE 5.5 The Inflation-Adjusted Value of the Minimum Wage Has Fallen by a Third from Its Peak

2. Using the analysis checklist, answer each question for this principle. Remember that for a yes answer, you should feel more than 70% confident, and then it's a YES. Otherwise, answer it as a NO. The answers should give you indicators on what is wrong with this chart and what needs correction.

Function – Cairo: The Functional Art – Art vs. Clarity

- Does the chart inform more than entertain?

- Can the visual be classified as informational only rather than beautiful art?

- Does information clarity take precedence over making a beautiful chart?

- In your judgment is the chart more informational than a piece of art?

- Does the visual appeal mostly to judgment rather than to the emotions?

Is the chart functionally informational rather than beautiful art?

3. Now, look at the aspects of this dimension that you scored as deficient (scored a NO). Based on the Function principles you learned in the companion class, what can you do to improve the chart?

Expert Solution

An expert may score this chart along the Function dimension as:

Function - Cairo: The Functional Art - Art vs. Clarity	Yes	No
Does the chart inform more than entertain?	x	
Can the visual be classified as informational only rather than beautiful art?	x	
Does information clarity take precedence over making the chart look beautiful?	x	
In your judgment is the chart more informational than a piece of art?	x	
Does the visual appeal mostly to judgment rather than to the emotions?	x	
The chart is functionally informational rather than beautiful art	5	
	100%	

The major point here is that the chart is very functional. No effort has been made to make it ornate or adorn it with any artistic elements. It would not win any data-as-art contests. We may need to dramatize it a bit, as we discuss in other sections.

4. As an additional exercise, consider the fourth chart (Figure 5.6) in the case study. Analyze it along the Function dimension.

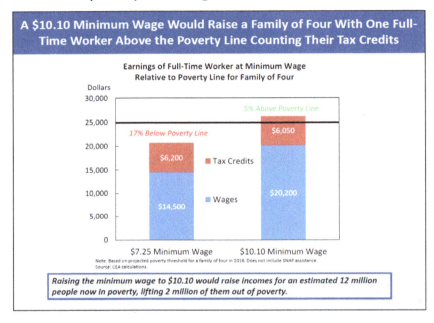

FIGURE 5.6 A $10.10 Minimum Wage Would Raise a Family of Four with One Full-Time Worker above the Poverty Line Counting Their Tax Credits

5. Using the analysis checklist, answer each question for this principle. Remember that for a yes answer, you should feel more than 70% confident, and then it's a YES. Otherwise, answer it as a NO. The answers should give you indicators on what is wrong with this chart and what needs correction.

Function – Cairo: The Functional Art – Art vs. Clarity

- Does the chart inform more than entertain?

- Can the visual be classified as informational only rather than beautiful art?

- Does information clarity take precedence over making a beautiful chart?

- In your judgment is the chart more informational than a piece of art?

- Does the visual appeal mostly to judgment rather than to the emotions?

Is the chart functionally informational rather than beautiful art?

6. Now, look at the aspects of this dimension that you scored as deficient (scored a NO). Based on the Function principles you learned in the companion class, what can you do to improve the chart?

CHAPTER 6

PURPOSE

Design with Purpose

Stephen Kosslyn, in *Graph Design for the Eye and Mind*, explains that we must evaluate the usefulness of a graph by how well we accounted for the context of the graph, the questions the reader must answer, and the nature of the audience. We must keep in mind who our audience is, what they want and need to know, and what key, framed analytical questions we answered in our analysis to inform them.

Information Need

We use our presentation and its embedded graphs to fulfill the needs of the requester and the organization. We should make sure our visuals fulfill an organizational, informational need. We should only be bringing data that is vital to the organization and its mission. We should also consider if the requester will be satisfied with this level of information and the news you bring. And most important, does the visual help them make a decision? In other words, does it educate your requester and audience sufficiently to satisfy their needs?

Max Shron, in his powerful *Thinking with Data*, presents a framework for defining data projects, including what data to collect, how to approach, organize, and analyze the results, and observing patterns of reasoning that help unveil the real problem that needs to be solved.

In his model, he explains how we can ascertain what an information need is. Here we will use our common sense and assume the analyst has done the analysis and has clearly determined what the information need is. At the point of communicating results, we need to be sure our visuals address that need. Usually, the need is about making a decision, often about a gap in the performance of some key performance indicator. Your graph should help the audience have sufficient information to know what to do. We bring our audience information to make an informed decision.

> *For a data visualization to be most successful, we must make sure the chart fulfills organizational information needs.*

Audience

Together with the audience's information needs, we should consider all other aspects of our viewers and listeners. What are their biases, what journey are they on, and what will they do with the information? Then we must match the visual style to the audience's biases, needs, and journey. The visual must take into consideration their point of view and account for their biases, education, and training. It should help them with their journey to make their numbers. Any mismatch would introduce noise, and the audience would perhaps confuse and miss the point you are making.

> *For a data visualization to be most successful, it should account for audience biases, needs, and journeys.*

Answer Well-Framed Analytical Questions

In the end, to satisfy the information need, we must present our results of answering well-framed analytical questions stemming from those needs. The analytical questions were posed and answered as part of the analysis process. The creation of the communication set of visuals is not the time to discover or search for the answers. We select, out of the many analytical questions we used to inform ourselves of the answers, those few that are the most important. They contain the key evidence, the facts, that support our conclusions. Those key facts must pop out of our visuals as clearly evident. But the basis of the visuals is bringing our audience the very best evidence supporting the conclusions, which will lead to action.

> *For a data visualization to be most successful, it should be the answer to a key, well-framed analytical question.*

The Exercises

The next three exercises in this lab help you practice analyzing charts along these three dimensions. There are two well-worked-out exercises. Make sure to use the tool in the accompanying spreadsheet. Fill it out as you go along. In the end, after you have gone through the eighteen exercises, you can see what the aggregate scores are in the summary tab.

Go through each exercise in the section and check yourself against the expert's opinion. Pay particular attention to where you and the expert disagree. Look at why the expert selected the answer they did and their rationale. Also, try to improve the chart along these dimensions. Again, check yourself against the expert's opinion.

You can reinforce your skills by doing each exercise for a second chart, as outlined in the manual. Once you are done with that, select any other chart in the case study set (see the end of the lab manual for more charts).

NOTE *You may reinforce these principles by watching the video tutorials on these topics found in the companion files on the disc or by downloading them from the publisher by writing to info@merclearning.com.*

Exercise 7: Information Needs

1. Consider the first chart (Figure 6.1) in the case study. Analyze it along the Need dimension.

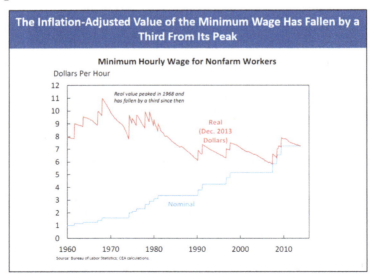

FIGURE 6.1 The Inflation-Adjusted Value of the Minimum Wage Has Fallen by a Third from Its Peak

2. Using the analysis checklist, answer each question for this principle. Remember that for a yes answer, you should feel more than 70% confident, and then it's a YES. Otherwise, answer it as a NO. The answers should give you indicators on what is wrong with this chart and what needs correction.

Need – Needs of the requester and the organization

- Does the visual fulfill an organizational information need?

- Is this data vital to the organization and its mission?

- Do you think the requester will be satisfied with this level of information and the news it brings?

- Does the visual help them make a decision?

- Does the visual educate the requester and the audience and meet their needs?

Does the chart fulfill organizational information needs?

3. Now, look at the aspects of this dimension that you scored as deficient (scored as a NO). Based on the Need principles you learned in the companion class, what can you do to improve the chart?

Expert Solution

An expert may score this chart along the Need dimension as:

Need- Needs of the requester and the organization	Yes	No
Does the visual fulfill an organizational information need?	x	
Is this data vital to the organization and their mission?	x	
Do you think the requester will be satisfied with this level of information and the news it brings?	x	
Does the visual help them make a decision?		x
Does the visual educate the requester and the audience and satisfies their needs?	x	
The chart fulfills organizational information needs	4	
	80%	

The chart does fulfill the purpose of the Council of Economic Advisors to inform policymakers and the general public. Most requesters will be satisfied with this information as accurate and pertinent to decisions they have to make to either (a) make policy or (b) be informed to advocate for or against policies. But, as pointed out earlier, the dramatic decrease in the buying power as a ratio is lost by leaving out a major signal, the ratio, which would be a more compelling fact that the information as presented.

4. As an additional exercise, consider the fourth chart (Figure 6.2) in the case study. Analyze it along the Need dimension.

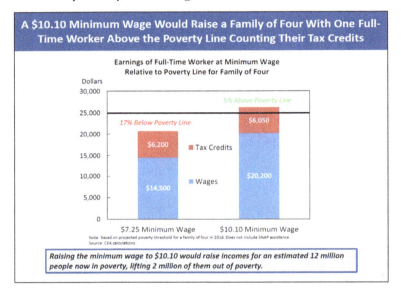

A $10.10 Minimum Wage Would Raise a Family of Four With One Full-Time Worker Above the Poverty Line Counting Their Tax Credits

Earnings of Full-Time Worker at Minimum Wage
Relative to Poverty Line for Family of Four

5% Above Poverty Line

17% Below Poverty Line

$6,050

$6,200

■ Tax Credits

$20,200

■ Wages

$14,500

$7.25 Minimum Wage $10.10 Minimum Wage

Note: Based on projected poverty threshold for a family of four in 2016. Does not include SNAP assistance.
Source: CEA calculations.

Raising the minimum wage to $10.10 would raise incomes for an estimated 12 million people now in poverty, lifting 2 million of them out of poverty.

FIGURE 6.2 A $10.10 Minimum Wage Would Raise a Family of Four with One Full-Time Worker above the Poverty Line Counting Their Tax Credits

5. Using the analysis checklist, answer each question for this principle. Remember that for a yes answer, you should feel more than 70% confident, and then it's a YES. Otherwise, answer it as a NO. The answers should give you indicators on what is wrong with this chart and what needs correction.

Need – Needs of the requester and the organization

- Does the visual fulfill an organizational information need?
- Is this data vital to the organization and its mission?
- Do you think the requester will be satisfied with this level of information and the news it brings?
- Does the visual help them make a decision?

- Does the visual educate the requester and the audience and satisfy their needs?

Does the chart fulfill organizational information needs?

6. Now, look at the aspects of this dimension that you scored as deficient (scored as a NO). Based on the Need principles you learned in the companion class, what can you do to improve the chart?

Exercise 8: Audience Characteristics

1. Consider the first chart (Figure 6.3) in the case study. Analyze it along the Audience dimension.

FIGURE 6.3 The Inflation-Adjusted Value of the Minimum Wage Has Fallen by a Third from Its Peak

2. Using the analysis checklist, answer each question for this principle. Remember that for a yes answer, you should feel more than 70% confident, and then it's a YES. Otherwise, answer it as a NO. The answers should give you indicators on what is wrong with this chart and what needs correction.

Audience – Cairo: Audience needs, biases, and journey
- Does the visual style match the audience's biases and needs?
- Does the visual style match the audience's journey?
- Does the visual take into consideration their point of view?
- Does the visual take into account their biases, education, and training?
- Does the visual help them with their journey?
- Does the visual help the audience "make their numbers"?

Does the chart allow for audience biases, needs, and journeys?

3. Now, look at the aspects of this dimension that you scored as deficient (scored as a NO). Based on the Audience principles you learned in the companion class, what can you do to improve the chart?

Expert Solution

An expert may score this chart along the Audience dimension as:

Audience - Cairo: Audience needs, biases and journey	Yes	No
Does the visual style match the audience biases?		x
Does the visual style match the audience needs?		x
Does the visual style match the audience journey?		x
Does the visual take into consideration their point of view?		x
Does the visual take into account their biases, education, training?		x
Does the visual help them with their journey?	x	
Does the visual help the audience "make their numbers"?		x
The chart allows for audience biases, needs and journey	**1**	
	14%	

The major point is that this chart and the whole presentation are conflicted as to who the audience is. Is the council speaking to policymakers and economists, experts, who would immediately appreciate the import of the chart? If that is the case, very little additional work is needed. But are they talking to the general public? Since they would have difficulties seeing the implications, more work in simplifying the chart is needed. Emphasis on the dramatic decrease of the ratio of buying power to minimum wage, for example, would make it clearer to the lay audience. This chart could still serve both purposes and meet the audience's needs by adding some basic data elements: the ratio, for example.

4. As an additional exercise, consider the fourth chart (Figure 6.4) in the case study. Analyze it along the Audience dimension.

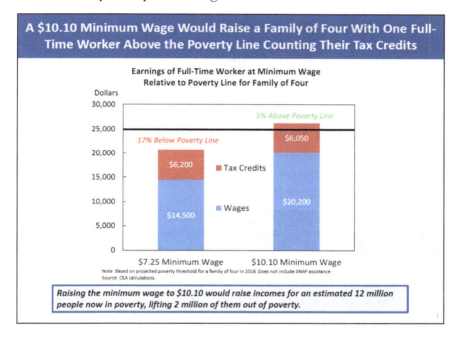

FIGURE 6.4 A $10.10 Minimum Wage Would Raise a Family of Four with One Full-Time Worker above the Poverty Line Counting Their Tax Credits

5. Using the analysis checklist, answer each question for this principle. Remember that for a yes answer, you should feel more than 70% confident, and then it's a YES. Otherwise, answer it as a NO. The answers should give you indicators on what is wrong with this chart and what needs correction.

Audience – Cairo: Audience needs, biases, and journey

- Does the visual style match the audience's biases and needs?

- Does the visual style match the audience's journey?

- Does the visual take into consideration their point of view?

- Does the visual take into account their biases, education, and training?

- Does the visual help them with their journey?

- Does the visual help the audience "make their numbers"?

Does the chart allow for audience biases, needs, and journeys?

6. Now, look at the aspects of this dimension that you scored as deficient (scored as a NO). Based on the Audience principles you learned in the companion class, what can you do to improve the chart?

Exercise 9: Framed Analytical Questions

1. Consider the first chart (Figure 6.5) in the case study. Analyze it along the Frame dimension.

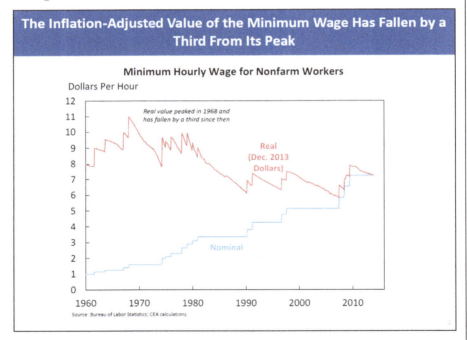

FIGURE 6.5 The Inflation-Adjusted Value of the Minimum Wage Has Fallen by a Third from Its Peak

2. Using the analysis checklist, answer each question for this principle. Remember that for a yes answer, you should feel more than 70% confident, and then it's a YES. Otherwise, answer it as a NO. The answers should give you indicators on what is wrong with this chart and what needs correction.

Frame – Shron: Thinking with Data CoNVO model

- Does the visual answer a well-framed analytical question stemming from an information need?

- Is the framed question evident from the visual?

- After seeing the visual, can the viewer express what the framed analytic question behind the visual is?

- Does the visual's title directly answer the framed question?

Does the visual answer a well-framed analytical question?

3. Now, look at the aspects of this dimension that you scored as deficient (scored as a NO). Based on the Frame principles you learned in the companion class, what can you do to improve the chart?

Expert Solution

An expert may score this chart along the Frame dimension as:

Frame - Shron: Thinking with Data CoNVO model	Yes	No
Does the visual answer a well framed analytical question stemming from an information need?	x	
Does the visual address and answer a well framed analytical question?	x	
Is the framed question evident from the visual?	x	
After seeing the visual can the viewer express what the framed analytic question behind the visual is?	x	
Does the visual's title directly answer the framed question?	x	
It it clear what point the visual is trying to make?	x	
The visual answers a well framed analytical question	6	
	100%	

The major point is that this chart does focus on the primary framed analytical questions: (a) what have been the increases in the minimum wage over the years, and (b) has that wage kept up with inflation by observing the concurrent decrease in buying power. No changes to the chart in this dimension need to be made.

4. As an additional exercise, consider the fourth chart (Figure 6.6) in the case study. Analyze it along the Storytellers dimension.

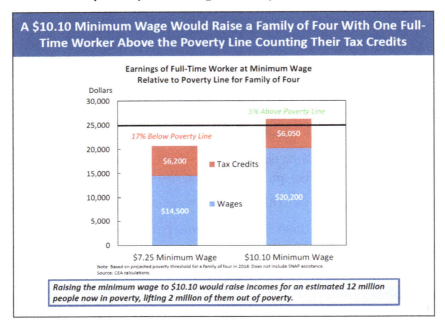

FIGURE 6.6 A $10.10 Minimum Wage Would Raise a Family of Four with One Full-Time Worker above the Poverty Line Counting Their Tax Credits

5. Using the analysis checklist, answer each question for this principle. Remember that for a yes answer, you should feel more than 70% confident, and then it's a YES. Otherwise, answer it as a NO. The answers should give you indicators on what is wrong with this chart and what needs correction.

Frame – Shron: Thinking with Data CoNVO model

- Does the visual answer a well-framed analytical question stemming from an information need?

- Is the framed question evident from the visual?

- After seeing the visual, can the viewer express what the framed analytic question behind the visual is?

- Does the visual's title directly answer the framed question?

- Is it clear what point the visual is trying to make?

Does the visual answer a well-framed analytical question?

6. Now, look at the aspects of this dimension that you scored as deficient (scored as a NO). Based on the Frame principles you learned in the companion class, what can you do to improve the chart?

CHAPTER 7

PERCEPTION

Perception

Henry David Thoreau, in his *Journal,* tells us that even though we "see" an object, it may not fully impress itself in our mind with its importance, and our mind will totally ignore it. It is because we are not looking for it, and thus we do not "see" it. He says that we only see the world we are looking for. His key admonition to us as data visualizers is to consider the question of not what the viewer sees, but what are they looking for? Looking happens in the mind; seeing happens in the eye.

What are we helping our audience to see and find?

Use the Eye-Brain System of Seeing

Alberto Cairo in *The Functional Art* writes that the right chart starts in the mind. We should try to understand how the mind makes sense of the world. Then we will be better able to anticipate the viewer. As Robert Spence has pointed out, visualization is not something that happens on a page or a screen; it happens in the mind. What we put down on the page or the screen is just an aid to produce insight.

By using Yarbus's work, we see that the eye is attracted unconsciously to strong focal point images. Therefore, the visual designer should decide the most important things you want your viewers to focus on and make them stand out when they first view the chart. They can use Gestalt principles, color theory, employment of the right chart, removing chart junk, and other methods to assist in focusing. You have to guide their viewing, so they get the point, almost unconsciously.

> *For a data visualization to be most successful, you must make sure that the eye of the viewer focuses on the most important point you are trying to make.*

Employ the Gestalt Principles of Perception

One way to assure that we are guiding the eye to the most important elements of the chart we have designed is to use the principles of the Gestalt psychology of perception. Have the principles been used to the greatest advantage? The most important principle for our purposes is to make sure the visual has good figure/ground differences. Does the main point visually stand out? Then we can consider secondary effects such as asking if the grouping has been used to the best effect. Has connectedness been used effectively? Has flow been used properly?

> *For a data visualization to be most successful, careful use of the principles of the Gestalt psychology of perception should be employed when creating the visual.*

Design with Quality

The architect Christopher Alexander has a unique perspective on quality, especially when it comes to designing something that must be useful to others. We shall consider our efforts at building charts as such and endeavor to be of use in informing others. On that premise, we can apply his formalism.

He tells us that a design can have a timeless quality, which is hard to define, but you see it, and you feel it when quality is there. He calls it the quality without a name. For a building, it is something that you are comfortable living in and being inside of; it is functional but also has its own beauty and fulfills a human need.

The human need in the matter of data visuals is to be informed. A visual will have that quality of being alive and being very useful to human beings if we use the principles Alexander outlines. It happens when the visual informs.

He tells us that the key element to building with quality is to use a pattern language, which is a collection of techniques that produce quality visuals—primarily, use all the good principles we outline here. Building with patterns resolves forces in tension and, in our case, brings knowledge. The tension in our case is between knowing and not knowing. So, the question we must answer positively is: does our visual resolve the tension in the viewer between not knowing (before seeing our visual) and knowing (after seeing our visual) and having their need satisfied? Is their ignorance dispelled? If we say yes, then we have a quality chart.

In other words, our visuals must be "alive." To be "alive," a visual must provide a service.

The service is the resolution of a tension the viewer brings to the chart. They want to know.

If the chart informs, the tension is relieved, and the viewer now "knows." If the viewer is still puzzled over the information after viewing, the chart does not have the living quality of informing and releasing the tension of ignorance.

For our chart to be effective, did it inform, did it relieve tension? Then we can say it is a quality chart.

The Exercises

The next three exercises in this lab help you practice analyzing charts along these three dimensions. There are two well-worked-out exercises. Make sure to use the tool in the accompanying spreadsheet. Fill it out as you go along. In the end, after you have gone through the eighteen exercises, you can see what the aggregate scores are in the summary tab.

Go through each exercise in the section and check yourself against the expert's opinion. Pay particular attention to where you and the expert disagree. Look at why the expert selected the answer they did and their rationale. Also, try to improve the chart along these dimensions. Again, check yourself against the expert's opinion.

You can reinforce your skills by doing each exercise for a second chart, as outlined in the manual. Once you are done with that, select any other chart in the case study set (see the end of the lab manual for more charts).

NOTE *A reminder all of the companion files and video tutorials for the exercises are available on the disc or for downloading by writing to the publisher at info@merclearning.com.*

Exercise 10: The Eye-Brain Connection

1. Consider the first chart (Figure 7.1) in the case study. Analyze it along the Seeing dimension.

FIGURE 7.1 The Inflation-Adjusted Value of the Minimum Wage Has Fallen by a Third from Its Peak

2. Using the analysis checklist, answer each question for this principle. Remember that for a yes answer, you should feel more than 70% confident, and then it's a YES. Otherwise, answer it as a NO. The answers should give you indicators on what is wrong with this chart and what needs correction.

Seeing – Anatomy: the human eye-brain system

- Is the eye of the viewer guided by chart elements to the important points?

- Does the eye of the viewer focus on the important points made by the visual?

- Does the viewer's eye go to the most important feature that needs to be stressed?

Does the eye of the viewer focus on the most important point being made?

3. Now, look at the aspects of this dimension that you scored as deficient (scored as a NO). Based on the Seeing principles you learned in the companion class, what can you do to improve the chart?

Expert Solution

An expert may score this chart along the Seeing dimension as:

Seeing – Anatomy: the human eye-brain system	Yes	No
Is the eye of the viewer guided by chart elements to the most important points?		x
Does the eye of the viewer focus on the most important points made by the visual?		x
Does the viewer's eye go to the most important feature that need to be stressed?	x	
The eye of the viewer focuses on the most important point being made		1
		33%

The major point is that the viewer's eye catches on the boxes with the notes, and they compete with the red line of the decrease in buying power. Making the buying power line red does focus the viewer on the most important elements on the chart. But it is too tenuous, and there is too much competing for attention, so the eye tends to wander all over the chart. The buying power line is too weak. Decrease the noise of the chart's other elements and emphasize the red line. More on that in the next section.

4. As an additional exercise, consider the fourth chart (Figure 7.2) in the case study. Analyze it along the Seeing dimension.

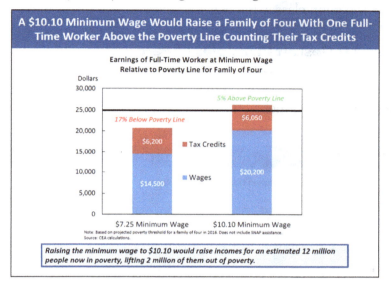

FIGURE 7.2 A $10.10 Minimum Wage Would Raise a Family of Four with One Full-Time Worker above the Poverty Line Counting Their Tax Credits

5. Using the analysis checklist, answer each question for this principle. Remember that for a yes answer, you should feel more than 70% confident, and then it's a YES. Otherwise, answer it as a NO. The answers should give you indicators on what is wrong with this chart and what needs correction.

Seeing – Anatomy: the human eye-brain system

- Is the eye of the viewer guided by chart elements to the important points?

- Does the eye of the viewer focus on the important points made by the visual?

- Does the viewer's eye go to the most important feature that needs to be stressed?

Does the eye of the viewer focus on the most important point being made?

6. Now, look at the aspects of this dimension that you scored as deficient (scored as a NO). Based on the Story principles you learned in the companion class, what can you do to improve the chart?

Exercise 11: Gestalt Principles of Perception

1. Consider the first chart (Figure 7.3) in the case study. Analyze it along the Mind dimension.

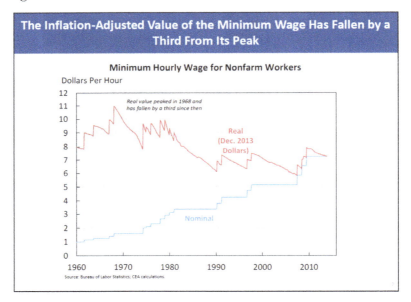

FIGURE 7.3 The Inflation-Adjusted Value of the Minimum Wage Has Fallen by a Third from Its Peak

2. Using the analysis checklist, answer each question for this principle. Remember that for a yes answer, you should feel more than 70% confident, and then it's a YES. Otherwise, answer it as a NO. The answers should give you indicators on what is wrong with this chart and what needs correction.

Mind – Gestalt: the psychology of perception

- Are basic Gestalt principles of perceptions used to the best advantage?
- Does the visual have good figure/ground differences?
- Has grouping been used effectively?
- Has connectedness been used effectively?
- Has flow been used effectively?

Have the principles of the Gestalt psychology of perception been thoughtfully employed in the visual?

3. Now, look at the aspects of this dimension that you scored as deficient (scored as a NO). Based on the Mind principles you learned in the companion class, what can you do to improve the chart?

Expert Solution

An expert may score this chart along the Mind dimension as:

Mind - Gestalt: psychology of perception	Yes	No
Are basic gestalt principles of perceptions been used to the best advantage?		x
Does the visual have good figure/ground differences?		x
Has grouping been used effectively?	x	
Has connectedness been used effectively?	x	
Has flow been used effectively?	x	
The principles of the Gestalt psychology of perception are thoughtfully employed in the visual	3	
	60%	

Some figure groundwork may be needed here, by graying out the axis to remove visual competition with the dramatic news of the data lines; making the data lines bolder; switching to scatter plot markers for the raises; lightening the color of the bars to the line plot for decreasing buying power; and perhaps adding a straight-line trend line for buying power superimposed to emphasize the dramatic loss on buying power.

4. As an additional exercise, consider the fourth chart (Figure 7.4) in the case study. Analyze it along the Mind dimension.

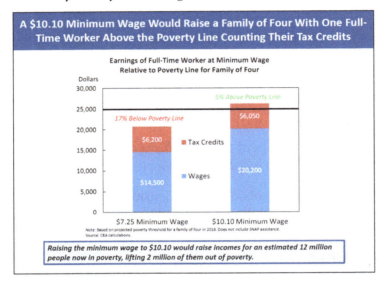

FIGURE 7.4 A $10.10 Minimum Wage Would Raise a Family of Four with One Full-Time Worker above the Poverty Line Counting Their Tax Credits

5. Using the analysis checklist, answer each question for this principle. Remember that for a yes answer, you should feel more than 70% confident, and then it's a YES. Otherwise, answer it as a NO. The answers should give you indicators on what is wrong with this chart and what needs correction.

Mind – Gestalt: the psychology of perception

- Are basic Gestalt principles of perception used to the best advantage?

- Does the visual have good figure/ground differences?

- Has grouping been used effectively?

- Has connectedness been used effectively?

- Has flow been used effectively?

Have the principles of the Gestalt psychology of perception been thoughtfully employed in the visual?

6. Now, look at the aspects of this dimension that you scored as deficient (scored as a NO). Based on the Mind principles you learned in the companion class, what can you do to improve the chart?

Exercise 12: Quality Matters

1. Consider the first chart (Figure 7.5) in the case study. Analyze it along the Quality dimension.

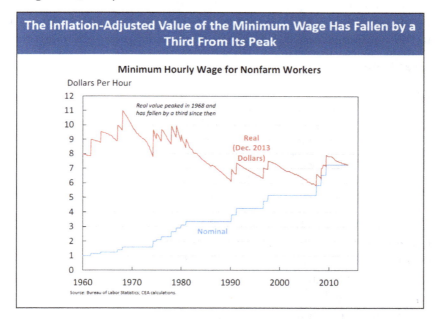

FIGURE 7.5 The Inflation-Adjusted Value of the Minimum Wage Has Fallen by a Third from Its Peak

2. Using the analysis checklist, answer each question for this principle. Remember that for a yes answer, you should feel more than 70% confident, and then it's a YES. Otherwise, answer it as a NO. The answers should give you indicators on what is wrong with this chart and what needs correction.

Quality – Alexander: Quality Without a Name

- Does the visual contain a quality that resolves the viewer's desire to be informed?

- Does the viewer walk away from the chart informed?

- Do the forces in tension (ignorance vs. knowing) find resolution in the chart?

- Is the tension of the viewer's ignorance relieved by how the information is presented?

Does the visual inform the viewer and dispel his ignorance?

3. Now, look at the aspects of this dimension that you scored as deficient (scored as a NO). Based on the Quality principles you learned in the companion class, what can you do to improve the chart?

Expert Solution

An expert may score this chart along the Quality dimension as:

Quality - Alexander: Quality Without a Name	Yes	No
Does the visual contain a quality that resolves the viewer's desire to be informed?		x
Does the viewer walk away from the chart informed?		x
Do the forces in tension (ignorance vs. knowing) find resolution in the chart?		x
Is the tension of viewer's ignorance relived by how the information is presented?		x
The visual informs and dispels ignorance	0	
	0%	

The major point here is that the viewer probably comes to the chart knowing what the minimum wage currently is, maybe even in a general way. But they want to know what it is now. Then they are confronted by the chart with the stark reality that even though the minimum wage has been going up and should continue to do so, its real worth has been dramatically decreased. It's the buying power that matters more than the actual amount. This chart does not hammer that point home enough. The short time a viewer gets with this chart in a presentation, or even viewing it as a report, may or may not convey the import of what we are telling them. The real danger is that the viewer walks away, still ignorant of the burning issue, the dramatic consequences of the minimum increases in the minimum wage.

To fix this chart in this dimension, the use of techniques to emphasize this point more dramatically is indicated.

4. As an additional exercise, consider the fourth chart (Figure 7.6) in the case study. Analyze it along the Quality dimension.

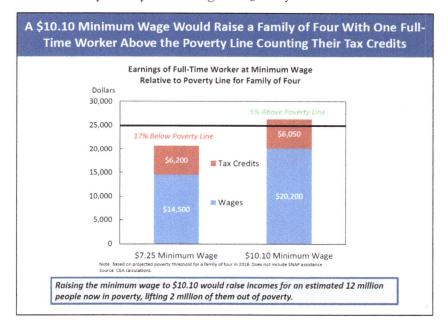

FIGURE 7.6 A $10.10 Minimum Wage Would Raise a Family of Four with One Full-Time Worker above the Poverty Line Counting Their Tax Credits

5. Using the analysis checklist, answer each question for this principle. Remember that for a yes answer, you should feel more than 70% confident, and then it's a YES. Otherwise, answer it as a NO. The answers should give you indicators on what is wrong with this chart and what needs correction.

Quality – Alexander: Quality Without a Name

- Does the visual contain a quality that resolves the viewer's desire to be informed?

- Does the viewer walk away from the chart informed?

- Do the forces in tension (ignorance vs. knowing) find resolution in the chart?

- Is the tension of the viewer's ignorance relieved by how the information is presented?

Does the visual inform the viewer and dispel his ignorance?

6. Now, look at the aspects of this dimension that you scored as deficient (scored as a NO). Based on the Quality principles you learned in the companion class, what can you do to improve the chart?

CHAPTER 8

METHOD

Method

We must use color appropriately, make sure our charts are devoid of all visual noise, and make sure the PowerPoint slide has a title that gets to the point of your message.

Use Color Effectively

Color should be used judiciously. It really enhances the chart. But if you use Excel, for example, the program chooses which colors to display based on some internal formula. That does not always lead to the best color combination.

First, you must use color sparsely. Most of your chart should be in black and white. Color should be left for those elements you want to draw to the viewer's attention. For example, you could gray out the axis somewhat to make it fade into the background. Does your use of color grab the viewer's attention?

Color should also be used in a way that is semantically correct. For example, is your data line for the United States as blue and for China as red, or in reverse? One is correct, and the other makes the viewer stop and pause to wonder what you mean by having it in a different color scheme than expected. That makes the viewers waste time absorbing your meaning, and you may even lose them.

Also, be aware that some people suffer from color dysfunctions in their eyesight (color blindness, for example), and your color scheme should account for that.

> *For a business data visual to be the most successful, color should be used judiciously and sparsely.*

Remove All Chart Junk

Richard Tufte is a prime mover in helping us understand that chart junk detracts from the viewer's comprehension of our charts. Just as we must declutter when we prepare our family home to be sold, clear up the viewing space in a visual as much as possible. Be ruthless. Use the redo and undo function in your chart maker. Put the feature in and then delete it. Go back and forth, putting it in and taking it out repeatedly to determine if valuable information would be lost if it was not there. Is there a simpler way to make that point?

Tufte uses the term chart junk for unnecessary or confusing visual elements in charts and graphs. Any markings and visual elements can be called chart junk if they are not part of the minimum set of visuals necessary to communicate the information understandably.

> *For a data visualization to be most successful, the visual should be clear of unnecessary visual elements that do not help the viewer understand.*

Tell the Story with the Title

Our friends at McKinsey and Company, the world-famous consulting powerhouse, have a wonderful practice in titling their presentation slides. The title of the slide (or even the visual, but not both) makes the business point of the graph explicitly. It tells them what the graph means right in the title. They don't let the viewers try to figure it out for themselves. They may draw an incorrect conclusion. You need to tell them, right there, at the top of your slide. Be succinct but express it as a complete thought; a phrase will suffice.

Charts should also have direct labeling for series. Avoid using a legend that makes the viewer's eye go back and forth and get lost as they try to get the point. Tell them directly what each chart feature is.

> *For a data visualization to be most successful, the title of the chart should convey the point you are trying to make by using the chart.*

The Exercises

The next three exercises in this lab help you practice analyzing charts along these three dimensions. There are two well-worked-out exercises. Make sure to use the tool in the accompanying spreadsheet. Fill it out as you go along. In the end, after you have gone through the eighteen exercises, you can see what the aggregate scores are in the summary tab.

Go through each exercise in the section and check yourself against the expert's opinion. Pay particular attention to where you and the expert disagree. Look at why the expert selected the answer they did and their rationale. Also, try to improve the chart along these dimensions. Again, check yourself against the expert's opinion.

You can reinforce your skills by doing each exercise for a second chart, as outlined in the manual. Once you are done with that, select any other chart in the case study set (see the end of the lab manual for more charts or refer to the companion files on the disc).

NOTE *You may reinforce these principles by watching the video tutorials on these topics found in the companion files on the disc or by downloading them from the publisher by writing to info@merclearning.com.*

Exercise 13: Using Color

1. Consider the first chart (Figure 8.1) in the case study. Analyze it along the Color dimension.

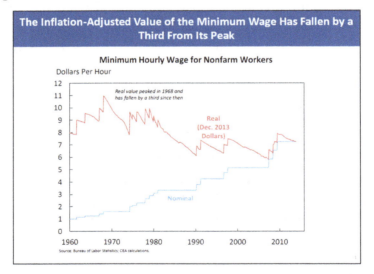

FIGURE 8.1 The Inflation-Adjusted Value of the Minimum Wage Has Fallen by a Third from Its Peak

2. Using the analysis checklist, answer each question for this principle. Remember that for a yes answer, you should feel more than 70% confident, and then it's a YES. Otherwise, answer it as a NO. The answers should give you indicators on what is wrong with this chart and what needs correction.

Color – Use of color, dysfunctions

- Has color been used judiciously and sparsely?

- Is the use of color semantically correct?

- Does the use of color grab the viewer's attention?

- Is color used to differentiate crossing elements?

- Is color used in area charts sparsely?

- Is color used to highlight results in tables sparsely?

Is color used judiciously and sparsely?

3. Now, look at the aspects of this dimension that you scored as deficient (scored as a NO). Based on the Color principles you learned in the companion class, what can you do to improve the chart?

Expert Solution

An expert may score this chart along the Color dimension as:

Color - Use of color, dysfunctions	Yes	No
Has color been used judiciously and sparsely?	x	
Is the use color semantically correct?	x	
Does the use of color grab the viewer's attention?	x	
Is color used to differentiate crossing elements?	x	
Is color used in area charts sparsely?	x	
Is color used to highlight results in tables sparsely?	x	
Color is used judiciously and sparsely	6	
	100%	

The major point here is that the decreasing buying power of the minimum wage is an alarming trend and is indicated by the red line, which is the one that indicates danger, that something has to change. Making the line blue suggests that the trend is not that important.

The color scheme is good: red, white, and blue, very American. The red and blue lines over the white background lend gravitas to an informational slide by the federal government.

A suggestion is that only one color fix may be needed: lower the voice of the axis and axis labels by 50% to focus the attention more on the data lines.

4. As an additional exercise, consider the fourth chart (Figure 8.2) in the case study. Analyze it along the Color dimension.

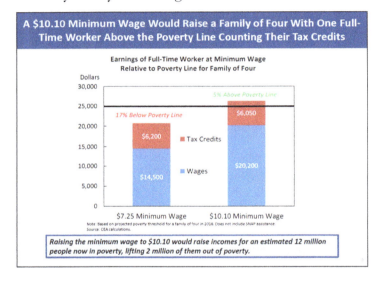

FIGURE 8.2 A $10.10 Minimum Wage Would Raise a Family of Four with One Full-Time Worker above the Poverty Line Counting Their Tax Credits

5. Using the analysis checklist, answer each question for this principle. Remember that for a yes answer, you should feel more than 70% confident, and then it's a YES. Otherwise, answer it as a NO. The answers should give you indicators on what is wrong with this chart and what needs correction.

Color – Use of color, dysfunctions

- Has color been used judiciously and sparsely?

- Is the use of color semantically correct?

- Does the use of color grab the viewer's attention?

- Is color used to differentiate crossing elements?
- Is color used in area charts sparsely?
- Is color used to highlight results in tables sparsely?

Is color used judiciously and sparsely?

6. Now, look at the aspects of this dimension that you scored as deficient (scored as a NO). Based on the Color principles you learned in the companion class, what can you do to improve the chart?

Exercise 14: Chart Junk

1. Consider the first chart (Figure 8.3) in the case study. Analyze it along the Chart Junk dimension.

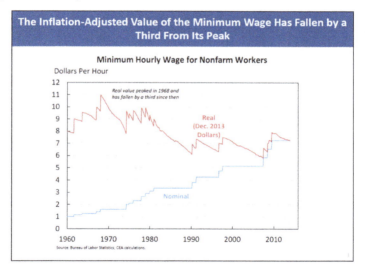

FIGURE 8.3 The Inflation-Adjusted Value of the Minimum Wage Has Fallen by a Third from Its Peak

2. Using the analysis checklist, answer each question for this principle. Remember that for a yes answer, you should feel more than 70% confident, and then it's a YES. Otherwise, answer it as a NO. The answers should give you indicators on what is wrong with this chart and what needs correction.

Chart Junk – Tufte: Chart junk

- Has all chart junk been removed?

- Has the data-to-ink ratio been properly balanced?

- Have all unnecessary elements been removed, including grid elements?

- Have all unnecessary elements been removed, including extra zeroes in the axis labels?

- Have all unnecessary extra bars been removed (could you have used a bullet chart format)?

- Have unnecessary pie chart sections been removed (not more than five)?

- Has area coloring that detracts been removed?

- Have unnecessary icons and other images been removed?

- Does the chart have sufficient drama?

Is the visual clear of unnecessary visual elements not leading to a clear point being made?

3. Now, look at the aspects of this dimension that you scored as deficient (scored as a NO). Based on the Chart Junk principles you learned in the companion class, what can you do to improve the chart?

Expert Solution

An expert may score this chart along the Chart Junk dimension as:

Chart Junk - Tufte: Chartjunk	Yes	No
Has all chart junk been removed?		x
Has the data to ink ratio been properly balanced?	x	
Have all unnecessary elements been removed, including grid elements?	x	
Have all unnecessary elements been removed, including extra zeroes in the axis labels	x	
Have all unnecessary extra bars been removed (could you have used a bullet chart format)?	x	
Have unnecessary pie chart sections been removed (not more than 5)?	x	
Has area coloring that detracts been removed?	x	
Have unnecessary icons and other images been removed?	x	
Does the chart have sufficient drama?		x
The visual is clear of unnecessary visual elements not leading to a clear point being made	7	
	78%	

The major point here is that most of the chart is very clean of chart junk. The boxed comments are distracting and may even be the main point of focus or perception when the viewer first sees the chart. Also, the voice of the axis could have been reduced (make them 50% gray?) to allow the viewer to focus on the data points.

We could fix this chart by moving the comments to the comment box at the bottom of the chart to make them inconspicuous. Also, gray out the axis, as mentioned previously. And the data lines could be thicker to add drama and guide the eye to the most important element: the dramatic difference and ominous trend in eroding buying power.

4. As an additional exercise, consider the fourth chart (Figure 8.4) in the case study. Analyze it along the Chart Junk dimension.

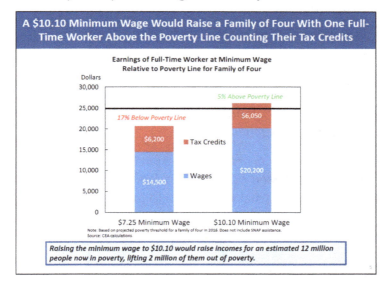

FIGURE 8.4 A $10.10 Minimum Wage Would Raise a Family of Four with One Full-Time Worker above the Poverty Line Counting Their Tax Credits

5. Using the analysis checklist, answer each question for this principle. Remember that for a yes answer, you should feel more than 70% confident, and then it's a YES. Otherwise, answer it as a NO. The answers should give you indicators on what is wrong with this chart and what needs correction.

Chart Junk – Tufte: Chart junk

- Has all chart junk been removed?

- Has the data-to-ink ratio been properly balanced?

- Have all unnecessary elements been removed, including grid elements?

- Have all unnecessary elements been removed, including extra zeroes in the axis labels?

- Have all unnecessary extra bars been removed (could you have used a bullet chart format)?

- Have unnecessary pie chart sections been removed (not more than five)?

- Has area coloring that detracts been removed?

- Have unnecessary icons and other images been removed?

- Does the chart have sufficient drama?

Is the visual clear of unnecessary visual elements not leading to a clear point being made?

6. Now, look at the aspects of this dimension that you scored as deficient (scored as a NO). Based on the Chart Junk principles you learned in the companion class, what can you do to improve the chart?

Exercise 15: Titling Charts

1. Consider the first chart (Figure 8.5) in the case study. Analyze it along the Title dimension.

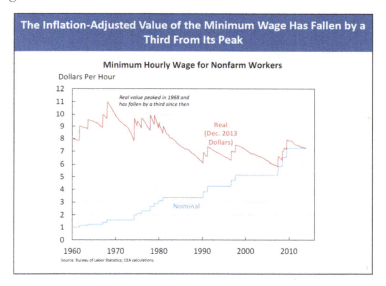

FIGURE 8.5 The Inflation-Adjusted Value of the Minimum Wage Has Fallen by a Third from Its Peak

2. Using the analysis checklist, answer each question for this principle. Remember that for a yes answer, you should feel more than 70% confident, and then it's a YES. Otherwise, answer it as a NO. The answers should give you indicators on what is wrong with this chart and what needs correction.

Title – McKinsey: A Better Way to Title Charts

- Does the title of the chart make the point directly?

- Does the title of the chart tell the story?

- Does the title of the chart answer the question being raised?

- Is the McKinsey method of titling used?

Does the title of the chart convey the point being made with the chart?

3. Now, look at the aspects of this dimension that you scored as deficient (scored as a NO). Based on the Title principles you learned in the companion class, what can you do to improve the chart?

Expert Solution

An expert may score this chart along the Title dimension as:

Title – McKinsey: A Better Way to Title Charts	Yes	No
Does the title of the chart makes the point directly?	x	
Does the title of the chart tell the story?	x	
Does the title of the chart answer the question being raised?	x	
Is the McKinsey method of titling used?	x	
The title of the chart conveys the point you are trying to make with the chart	4	
	100%	

The major point is that this chart seems to be properly titled using the McKinsey principle. Also, direct labeling is used, so it is good in that respect. Not much should change in this dimension.

4. As an additional exercise, consider the fourth chart (Figure 8.6) in the case study. Analyze it along the Title dimension.

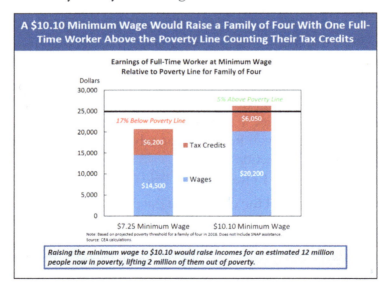

FIGURE 8.6 A $10.10 Minimum Wage Would Raise a Family of Four with One Full-Time Worker above the Poverty Line Counting Their Tax Credits

5. Using the analysis checklist, answer each question for this principle. Remember that for a yes answer, you should feel more than 70% confident, and then it's a YES. Otherwise, answer it as a NO. The answers should give you indicators on what is wrong with this chart and what needs correction.

Title – McKinsey: A Better Way to Title Charts

- Does the title of the chart make the point directly?

- Does the title of the chart tell the story?

- Does the title of the chart answer the question being raised?

- Is the McKinsey method of titling used?

Does the title of the chart convey the point being made with the chart?

6. Now, look at the aspects of this dimension that you scored as deficient (scored as a NO). Based on the Title principles you learned in the companion class, what can you do to improve the chart?

CHAPTER 9

CHARTS

Charts

In this last lab, we will experiment with selecting the right chart to match our purpose and story. We will also optimize tables so they can be used effectively in the short time they will be displayed during a presentation.

Use the Right Chart

The researchers Cleveland and McGill have developed a useful scale for elementary perceptual tasks, which we apply to decide the type of graph that should be used for the level of accuracy desired. Cleveland and McGill's functional scale tells us that the higher the encoding method, the more accurate the comparison it facilitates.

This scale should guide us to match the type of graph to use for the question being answering. Using this scale, we can ask: (a) Is the right chart being used for the intended purpose? (b) Does the visual use the right level of encoding for the level of accurate judgment desired? and (c) Does the chart type match the type of question being answered?

> *For a data visualization to be most successful, the type of chart used matches the level of judgment required.*

Select the Chart Type Effectively

For this lab, we should consider answering a few basic questions in the use of the chart type that was selected: (a) are the charts answering the right business question? (b) does the chart match the business question being presented? and (c) have the four basic chart types been used properly?

Each chart type is best suited to presenting answers to certain types of questions. For example, a Pareto chart is excellent for showing the 80/20% contributions for certain contributors. Pie charts are best for contributions to a whole. Match the point you are trying to make to the type of chart that suits that type of information best.

> *For a data visualization to be most successful, the chart type used matches the business question being answered.*

Enhance Table Data for Emphasis

In her blog, Storytelling with Data, Cole Nussbaumer Knaflic demonstrates how a focus on communication leads from a formatted table to a more intuitive view of key characteristics and elements within the dataset.

When using tables in our visuals, we must ask: are we using the table to analyze or to tell? Is the use of referenceable or glanceable visuals appropriate? Also, we must ask if the referenceable visual has been designed to be legible and readable. Do the tables have enough white space? Has shading of the table been used appropriately and sparingly? Has the emphasis been appropriately added with conditional formatting? And have thumbnail graphs such as Sparklines been employed to add insight?

> *For a data visualization to be most successful, have referenceable visuals (tables) made readable with appropriate conditional formatting and thumbnail graphs.*

The Exercises

The next three exercises in this lab help you practice analyzing charts along these three dimensions. There are two well-worked-out exercises. Make sure to use the tool in the accompanying spreadsheet. Fill it out as you go along. In the end, after you have gone through the eighteen exercises, you can see what the aggregate scores are in the summary tab.

Go through each exercise in the section and check yourself against the expert's opinion. Pay particular attention to where you and the expert disagree. Look at why the expert selected the answer they did and their rationale. Also, try to improve the chart along these dimensions. Again, check yourself against the expert's opinion.

You can reinforce your skills by doing each exercise for a second chart, as outlined in the manual. Once you are done with that, select any other chart in the case study set.

NOTE *You may reinforce these principles by watching the video tutorials on these topics found in the companion files on the disc or by downloading them from the publisher by writing to info@merclearning.com.*

Exercise 16: Using the Right Chart

1. Consider the first chart (Figure 9.1) in the case study. Analyze it along the Right Chart dimension.

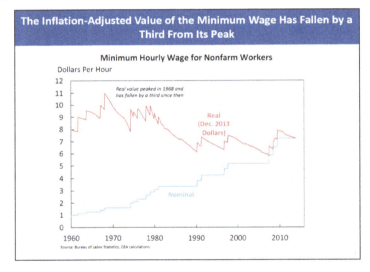

FIGURE 9.1 The Inflation-Adjusted Value of the Minimum Wage Has Fallen by a Third from Its Peak

2. Using the analysis checklist, answer each question for this principle. Remember that for a yes answer, you should feel more than 70% confident, and then it's a YES. Otherwise, answer it as a NO. The answers should give you indicators on what is wrong with this chart and what needs correction.

Right Chart – Cleveland and McGill: Functional Scale

- Is the right chart being used for the intended purpose?

- Does the visual use the right level of encoding for the level of accurate judgment desired?

- Does the chart type match the type of question being answered?

Does the type of chart being used match the level of judgment required?

3. Now, look at the aspects of this dimension that you scored as deficient (scored as a NO). Based on the Right Chart principles you learned in the companion class, what can you do to improve the chart?

Expert Solution

An expert may score this chart along the Right Chart dimension as:

Right Chart - Cleveland and McGill: Functional Scale	Yes	No
Is the right chart being used for the intended purpose?		x
Does the visual use the right level of encoding for the level of accurate judgment desired?		x
Does the chart type match the type of question being answered?		x
The type of chart used matches the level of judgement required	0	
	0%	

The major point here is that using a line chart for a time series at first blush seems like the right choice. But for the purpose of comparing the increases in the amount of the minimum wage to decreases to its buying power, there may be a better choice. A scatter plot with trend lines would be more effective, or a bar graph for minimum wage with a line chart of decreasing buying power might be more dramatic. Increases in the minimum wage are discrete and hold at a level for many years so that a bar would be great, perhaps without gaps. Since the cost of living changes year over year continuously, a line graph of its effect in eroding the buying power of the minimum wage would be more dramatic and effective.

4. As an additional exercise consider the fourth chart (Figure 9.2) in the case study. Analyze it along the Right Chart dimension.

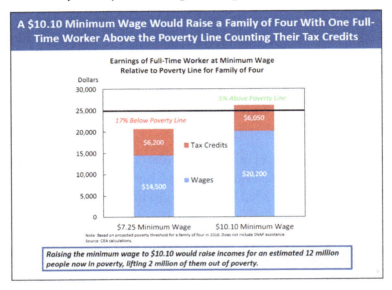

FIGURE 9.2 A $10.10 Minimum Wage Would Raise a Family of Four with One Full-Time Worker above the Poverty Line Counting Their Tax Credits

5. Using the analysis checklist, answer each question for this principle. Remember that for a yes answer, you should feel more than 70% confident, and then it's a YES. Otherwise, answer it as a NO. The answers should give you indicators on what is wrong with this chart and what needs correction.

Right Chart – Cleveland and McGill: Functional Scale

- Is the right chart being used for the intended purpose?

- Does the visual use the right level of encoding for the level of accurate judgment desired?

- Does the chart type match the type of question being answered?

Does the type of chart being used match the level of judgment required?

6. Now, look at the aspects of this dimension that you scored as deficient (scored as a NO). Based on the Right Chart principles you learned in the companion class, what can you do to improve the chart?

Exercise 17: Chart Selection

1. Consider the first chart (Figure 9.3) in the case study. Analyze it along the Selection dimension.

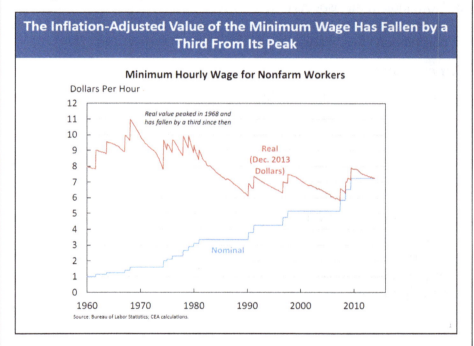

FIGURE 9.3 The Inflation-Adjusted Value of the Minimum Wage Has Fallen by a Third from Its Peak

2. Using the analysis checklist, answer each question for this principle. Remember that for a yes answer, you should feel more than 70% confident, and then it's a YES. Otherwise, answer it as a NO. The answers should give you indicators on what is wrong with this chart and what needs correction.

Selection – The Basic Charts

- Are your charts answering the right business question?

- Does the chart match the business question being presented?

- Have the basic four chart types been used properly?

Does the chart type used match the business question being answered?

3. Now, look at the aspects of this dimension that you scored as deficient (scored as a NO). Based on the Selection principles you learned in the companion class, what can you do to improve the chart?

Expert Solution

An expert may score this chart along the Selection dimension as:

Selection – The Basic Charts	Yes	No
Are your charts answering the right business question?	x	
Does the chart match the business question being presented?		x
Have the basic four chart types been used properly?		x
The chart type used matches the business question being answered	1	
	33%	

The major point, in this case, is that this is probably the right chart, as it is a question of trends over time and the display of time series, and thus a line chart. Further, the display of the line as a stepped display, although accurate in that the minimum wage increases discretely and stays constant between jumps, is not pleasing to the eye, and that choppiness distracts from the message. The viewer starts wondering what the choppiness means and then gets it after pondering it a while, but in the meantime, the speaker or presenter has lost the attention of the viewer.

And the expert suggests you would fix this chart by making a scatter plot of the new minimum wage at the time it went into effect vs. the date of that occurrence and then add a linear regression to emphasize the increase. Use the same for decreases in buying power over time. That would more effectively dramatize the stark difference between the two, which is the message of this chart.

4. As an additional exercise, consider the fourth chart (Figure 9.4) in the case study. Analyze it along the Selection dimension.

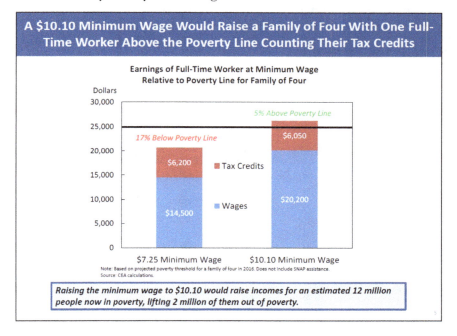

FIGURE 9.4 A $10.10 Minimum Wage Would Raise a Family of Four with One Full-Time Worker above the Poverty Line Counting Their Tax Credits

5. Using the analysis checklist, answer each question for this principle. Remember that for a yes answer, you should feel more than 70% confident, and then it's a YES. Otherwise, answer it as a NO. The answers should give you indicators on what is wrong with this chart and what needs correction.

Selection – The Basic Charts

- Are your charts answering the right business question?

- Does the chart match the business question being presented?

- Have the basic four chart types been used properly?

Does the chart type used match the business question being answered?

6. Now, look at the aspects of this dimension that you scored as deficient (scored as a NO). Based on the Selection principles you learned in the companion class, what can you do to improve the chart?

Exercise 18: Tables

1. Consider the first chart (Figure 9.5) in the case study. Analyze it along the Tables dimension.

FIGURE 9.5 The Inflation-Adjusted Value of the Minimum Wage Has Fallen by a Third from Its Peak

2. Using the analysis checklist, answer each question for this principle. Remember that for a yes answer, you should feel more than 70% confident, and then it's a YES. Otherwise, answer it as a NO. The answers should give you indicators on what is wrong with this chart and what needs correction.

Tables – Analyze or Tell?

- Is the use of a table appropriate in this case?
- Is the table readable?

- Do the tables have enough white space?

- Is the shading of the table used appropriately?

- Has appropriate emphasis been added to the table with conditional formatting?

- Have thumbnail graphs such as Sparklines been employed to add insight?

Are referenceable visuals (tables) readable with appropriate conditional formatting and thumbnail graphs used for emphasis?

3. Now, look at the aspects of this dimension that you scored as deficient (scored as a NO). Based on the Tables principles you learned in the companion class, what can you do to improve the chart?

Expert Solution

An expert may score this chart along the Selection dimension as:

Tables - Analyze or Tell?	Yes	No
Is the use of a table appropriate in this case?	x	
Is the table readable?	x	
Do the tables have enough white space?	x	
Is shading of the table used appropriately?	x	
Is appropriate emphasis been added to the table with conditional formatting?	x	
Have thumbnail graphs such as Sparklines been employed to add insight?	x	
Referenceable visuals (tables) are readable with appropriate conditional formatting and thumbnail graphs for emphasis	6	
	100%	

The major point is that this chart is not about a table. Plus, switching to a table may not have enhanced this chart at all to accomplish its purpose. If the purpose is to convince experts, data shown as a line chart makes sense, especially to demonstrate the sharp trends. For the general public, this information is better served as a simple set of numbers showing an increase in the amount for the minimum wage but a decrease in its buying power over a thirty-year span. A two-number comparison table or even an infographic might be more effective.

4. As an additional exercise, consider the fourth (Figure 9.6) chart in the case study. Analyze it along the Tables dimension.

FIGURE 9.6 A $10.10 Minimum Wage Would Raise a Family of Four with One Full-Time Worker above the Poverty Line Counting Their Tax Credits

5. Using the analysis checklist, answer each question for this principle. Remember that for a yes answer, you should feel more than 70% confident, and then it's a YES. Otherwise, answer it as a NO. The answers should give you indicators on what is wrong with this chart and what needs correction.

Tables – Analyze or Tell?

- Is the use of a table appropriate in this case?

- Is the table readable?

- Do the tables have enough white space?

- Is the shading of the table used appropriately?

- Has appropriate emphasis been added to the table with conditional formatting?

- Have thumbnail graphs such as Sparklines been employed to add insight?

Are referenceable visuals (tables) readable with appropriate conditional formatting and thumbnail graphs used for emphasis?

6. Now, look at the aspects of this dimension that you scored as deficient (scored as a NO). Based on the Tables principles you learned in the companion class, what can you do to improve the chart?

CASE STUDY DOCUMENT

NOTE *As a reminder, all of the companion files and video tutorials for the exercises are available on the disc or for downloading by writing to the publisher at info@merclearning.com.*

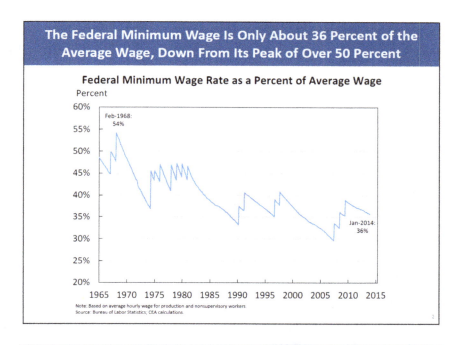

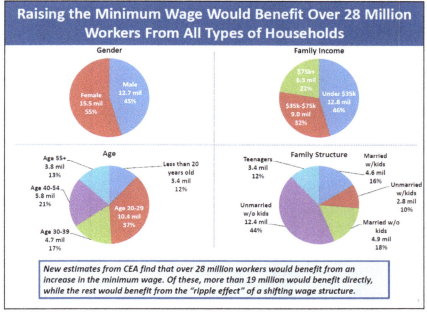

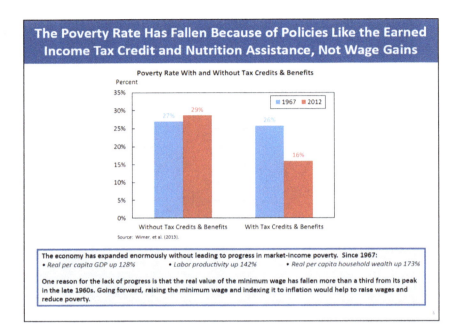

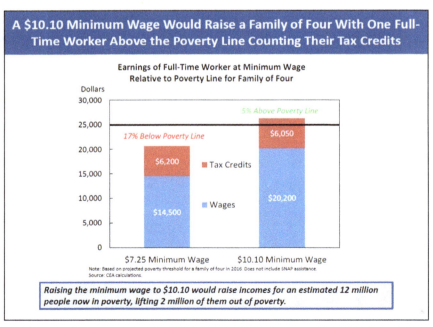

The Minimum Wage Affects Inequality – With Inequality Between Low/Middle-Income Historically Tracking the Minimum Wage

Women's 50-10 Wage Gap vs. Real Minimum Wage

Note: The 50-10 wage gap is the ratio of income earned at the 50th percentile to income earned at the 10th percentile.
Source: CEA calculations based on updated data from Lemieux (2007).

Studies have shown that the minimum wage plays an important role in reducing inequality.
➢ Important in the bottom of the wage distribution and for women (DiNardo, Fortin, and Lemieux, 1996).
➢ Declining real value of the minimum wage explained roughly one-third to one-half of the increase in the 50-10 wage gap for women during the 1980s (Autor, Manning, and Smith, 2010).

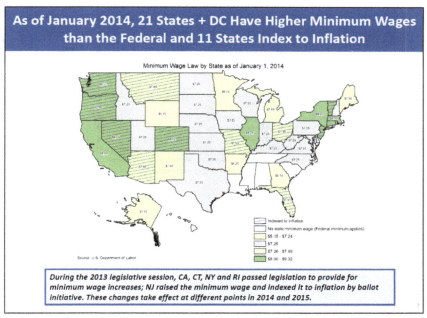

As of January 2014, 21 States + DC Have Higher Minimum Wages than the Federal and 11 States Index to Inflation

Minimum Wage Law by State as of January 1, 2014

Source: U.S. Department of Labor

During the 2013 legislative session, CA, CT, NY and RI passed legislation to provide for minimum wage increases; NJ raised the minimum wage and indexed it to inflation by ballot initiative. These changes take effect at different points in 2014 and 2015.

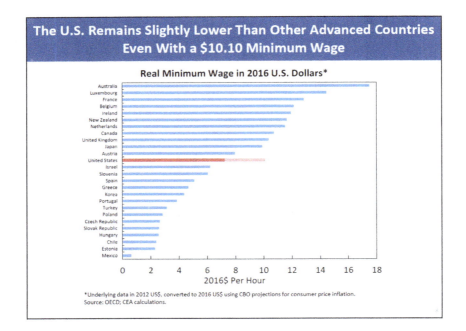

The U.S. Remains Slightly Lower Than Other Advanced Countries Even With a $10.10 Minimum Wage

Real Minimum Wage in 2016 U.S. Dollars*

*Underlying data in 2012 US$, converted to 2016 US$ using CBO projections for consumer price inflation.
Source: OECD; CEA calculations.

Raising the Minimum Wage Would Help Businesses by Increasing Productivity and Reducing Turnover and Absenteeism

Some of the key findings from decades of research on the minimum wage:

1. **Increases worker productivity.** A higher minimum wage would increase the productivity of workers:
   - Greater motivation and perception of fairness. Workers are motivated directly by feeling they are receiving a fair wage (e.g., Bewley 1999; Mas 2006). Akerlof (1986) argues that higher wages increase employee morale, which raises productivity. Also, workers monitor each other more when they feel that they are receiving good, fair wages, creating a culture of hard work that allows employers to spend less on supervising them (Akerlof 2012).
   - Improved focus on the job. Higher wages help workers maintain better physical and mental health and could help relieve "decision fatigue" (Mani, et al 2013; Shah et al, 2012), allowing them to be more productive at work.

2. **Reduces turnover and saves on recruiting/training costs.** Higher wages lead to lower turnover, reducing the amount employers must spend recruiting and training new employees (Dube, Reich, and Naidu 2005; Dube, Lester, and Reich 2013).

3. **Reduces absenteeism.** When workers are paid higher wages, they are absent from work less often, increasing both their own productivity and that of their coworkers (Allen 1983; Mefford 1986; Pfeifer 2010; Zhang 2013).

Based on 64 Studies of Minimum Wage Increases, Researchers Find "No Discernable Effect on Employment"

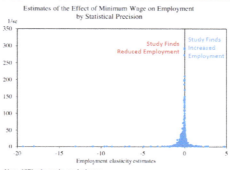

Estimates of the Effect of Minimum Wage on Employment
by Statistical Precision

Note: "SE" refers to the standard error.
Source: Doucouliagos and Stanley (2009); data provided by John Schmitt.

Studies have shown that minimum wage increases lead to "little or no employment response":
➢ Comparing 288 pairs of contiguous U.S. counties with minimum wage differentials from 1990 to 2006 finds "no adverse employment effects" (Dube, Lester, and Reich, 2010).
➢ A meta-analysis of the minimum wage research published since 2000 concludes, "The weight of that evidence points to little or no employment response to modest increases in the minimum wage" (Schmitt, 2013).
➢ Researchers have noted that even this distribution of studies is biased because studies (spuriously) finding large positive effects on employment are likely not to be published while studies (spuriously) finding large negative effects on employment are published.

APPENDIX: Beneficiaries of Increasing the Minimum Wage

Characteristics of Minimum Wage Workers and Workers Affected by Increasing the Federal Minimum Wage

	Minimum Wage Workers	Workers Affected by Increase to $10.10	All Workers		Minimum Wage Workers	Workers Affected by Increase to $10.10	All Workers
% of All Workers	4.5%	21.4%	100.0%	**Family Structure**			
				Married w/ kids	12.7%	16.3%	26.6%
Sex				Unmarried w/ kids	9.0%	10.0%	7.5%
Male	42.1%	45.0%	51.5%	Married w/o kids	12.9%	17.4%	27.4%
Female	57.9%	55.0%	48.5%	Unmarried w/o kids	41.2%	44.2%	35.1%
				Teenagers	24.2%	12.1%	3.4%
Family Income							
Under $35,000	47.7%	45.5%	24.8%	**Age**			
$35k-$75k	30.2%	32.1%	35.0%	Under 20 yrs old	24.2%	12.1%	3.4%
$75k+	22.2%	22.4%	40.2%	Age 20-29	35.4%	37.0%	21.9%
				Age 30-39	13.9%	16.7%	21.7%
Race/Ethnicity				Age 40-54	16.0%	20.6%	33.0%
White	52.3%	53.3%	65.0%	Age 55+	10.4%	13.6%	19.9%
Black	13.0%	14.5%	11.2%				
Hispanic	27.6%	25.2%	16.2%				
Asian	4.7%	4.8%	5.8%				
Other	2.4%	2.3%	1.8%				

Source: Current Population Survey, outgoing rotation groups for December 2012 through November 2013. Minimum Wage Workers earn a wage within 25 cents above or below the federal minimum of $7.25. Affected workers earn a wage between 25 cents below the minimum and $10.10, deflated from 2016 dollars to 2013 dollars using CBO projections. Percentages may not sum to 100% within category due to rounding.

CHAPTER 11

CASE STUDY SOLUTION – AN EXPERT OPINION

The Six Dimensions

We analyzed the chart in six dimensions with three aspects each, making a total of eighteen directions of analysis:

Story Dimension	**Purpose Dimension**	**Method Dimension**
Visual Story	Need	Color
Visual Props	Audience	Chart Junk
Storytellers	Frame	Title

Sign Dimension	**Perception Dimension**	**Chart Dimension**
Sign	Seeing	Right Chart
Communication	Mind	Selection
Function	Quality	Tables

The Chart Being Analyzed

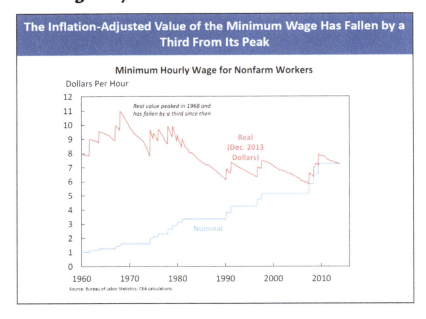

An Expert Point of View

Story Dimension

We will make a major assumption as the basis of our analysis: these charts were directed to government policymakers (staff of the executive and legislative branches, and state and municipal governments). We will take this chart as part of a story to convince policymakers of the importance of adopting higher minimum wage standards in the country through legislation and administrative action.

Visual Story

On that basis, the major points where the chart does not work is that although the title of the graph tells us the point of the graph, the picture is hard to decipher. The data is accurate and correct and is the right data to use and display, and the choice of the chart is probably a good one. Still, it does not show the major drop in the effective buying power of minimum wage over the years, even as the amount of the minimum wage has risen.

We suggest you would fix this chart by doing the following: perhaps using trend lines to show the stark rise in the amount of minimum wage while its buying power was dramatically decreasing. There must be a way to make that dramatic drop to be more evident. One gets lost in the meandering stepwise lines, accurate but not compelling.

We will assume that this set of slides is probably used by Council of Economic Advisors to brief policymakers on the policy initiative supported by the executive branch at the time.

Visual Props

The primary point appears to be that the Council of Economic Advisors is also using this set of slides as a briefing book on the issue. You can't have it both ways. If it is used as a briefing book, the charts may be more detailed as these are. If used as props for a presentation, they need to be more compelling and less technical.

We suggest you would fix this chart by doing the following: use these slides as a basis for a more compelling set of charts and select better chart types, especially for this particular chart, that make the point better.

Storytellers

The major point is that there is probably a better, more compelling chart form, such as Playfair's iconic bar graphs.

We suggest you would fix this chart by changing to a bar chart, for example, that accentuates the upward flow of the minimum wage over the years versus the downward loss of its buying power.

Sign Dimension

Sign

The major point is that the designers of the chart did make a clear sign that the buying power of the minimum wage has been decreasing dramatically over the years, while seemingly the amount of the minimum wage has been increasing. The viewer has to study the chart for a while to infer this conclusion. Even though the title tells the story, the data does not easily support the message. No clear sign has been given. Again, the designers are probably speaking to economists, technical people who easily derive this knowledge from the chart given.

We suggest you would fix this chart by making the drop in buying power over time more obvious.

Communication

The major point is that the important signal is the dramatic decrease in the buying power of the minimum wage. We see that the minimum wage and its buying power are equal at the right of the chart, which could send a signal that all is well, that it is good that buying power and minimum wage are equal. What is dramatic is the ratio of the minimum wage to buying power. At the start of the chart it is 8:1, and the end it is 1:1. It takes a while for the reader or viewer to come to this startling fact. That is the premise for making a case for a raise in the minimum wage, no? That signal is lost by presenting the data flat, and not in a meaningful way.

Other than that, the chart is very clear and the noise is minimized, and only one point is being made.

We could fix this chart by adding a line of the ratio of buying power to minimum wage.

Function

The major point here is that the chart is very functional. No effort has been made to make it ornate or adorn it with any artistic elements. It would not win any data-as-art contests. We may need to dramatize it a bit, as we discuss in other sections.

Purpose Dimension

Need

The chart does fulfill the purpose of the Council of Economic Advisors to inform policymakers and the general public. Most requesters will be satisfied with this information as accurate and pertinent to decisions they have to make to either (a) make policy or (b) be informed to advocate for or against policies. But, as pointed out earlier, the dramatic decrease in the buying power as a ratio is lost by leaving out a major signal, the ratio, which would be a more compelling fact than the information as presented.

Audience

The major point is that this chart and the whole presentation are conflicted as to who the audience is. Is the council speaking to policymakers and economists, experts, who would immediately appreciate the import of the chart? If that is the case, very little additional work is needed. But are they talking to the general public? Since they would have difficulties seeing the implications, more work in simplifying the chart is needed. Emphasis on the dramatic decrease of the ratio of buying power to minimum wage, for example, would make it clearer to the lay audience. This chart could still serve both purposes and meet the audience's needs by adding some basic data elements: the ratio, for example.

Frame

The major point is that this chart does focus on the primary framed analytical questions: (a) what have been the increases in the minimum wage over the years? and (b) has that wage kept up with inflation by observing the concurrent decrease in buying power? No changes to the chart in this dimension need to be made.

Perception Dimension

Seeing

The major point is that the viewer's eye catches on the boxes with the notes, and they compete with the red line of the decrease in buying power. Making the buying power line red does focus the viewer on the most important elements on the chart. But it is too tenuous, and there is too much competing for attention, so the eye tends to wander all over the chart. The buying power line is too weak. Decrease the noise of the other chart elements and emphasize the red line—more on that in the next section.

Mind

Some figure groundwork may be needed here, by graying out the axis to remove competition with the dramatic news of the data lines; making the data lines bolder; switching to scatter plot markers for the raises; lightening the color of the bars to the line plot for decreasing buying power; and perhaps adding a straight-line trend line for buying power superimposed to emphasize the dramatic loss on buying power.

Quality

The major point here is that the viewer probably comes to the chart knowing what the minimum wage currently is, maybe even in a general way. But they want to know what it is now. Then they are confronted by the chart with the stark reality that even though the minimum wage has been going up and should continue to do so, its real worth has been dramatically decreased. It's the buying power that matters more than the actual amount. This chart does not hammer that point home enough. The brief time the viewer gets to see this chart in a presentation, or even viewing it as a report, may or may not convey the import of what they are seeing. There is a real danger that the viewer walks away, still ignorant of the burning issue of the dramatic consequences of the minimum increases in the minimum wage.

To fix this chart in this dimension, the use of other techniques to emphasize this point more dramatically is indicated.

Method Dimension

Color

The major point here is that the decreasing buying power of the minimum wage is an alarming trend and is indicated by the red line, which is the one that indicates danger, that something must change. Making the line blue says that the trend is not that important.

The color scheme is good: red, white, and blue, very American. The red and blue lines over the white background lend gravitas to an informational slide by the federal government.

We suggest that only one color fix may be needed: lower the voice of the axis and axis labels by 50% to focus the attention more on the data lines.

Chart Junk

The major point is that most of the chart is very clean of chart junk. The boxed comments are distracting and may even be the main point of focus or perception when the viewer first sees the chart. Also, the voice of the axis could have been reduced (make them 50% gray?) to allow the viewer to focus on the data points. We could fix this chart by moving the comments to the comment box at the bottom of the chart to make them inconspicuous. Also, gray out the axis, as mentioned previously. And the data lines could be thicker to add drama and guide the eye to the most important element: the dramatic difference and ominous trend in eroding buying power.

Title

The major point is that this chart seems to be properly titled using the McKinsey principle. Also, direct labeling is used, so it is good in that respect. There is not much to change in this dimension.

Chart Dimension

Right Chart

The major point here is that using a line chart for a time series at first blush seems like the right choice. But for the purpose of comparing the increases in the amount of the minimum wage to decreases to its buying power, there may be a better choice. A scatter plot with trend lines would be more effective, or a bar graph for minimum wage with a line chart of decreasing buying power might be more dramatic. Increases in the minimum wage are discrete and hold at a level for many years, so that a bar graph would be great, perhaps without gaps. Since the cost of living changes continuously year over year, a line graph of its eroding effect of the buying power of the minimum wage would be more dramatic and effective.

Selection

The major point, in this case, is that this is probably the right chart, as it is a question of trends over time and the display of time series; thus a line chart. Further, the display of the line as a stepped display, although accurate in that the minimum wage increases discretely and stays constant between jumps, is not pleasing to the eye, and that choppiness distracts from the message. The viewer starts wondering what the choppiness means and then gets it after pondering it a while, but in the meantime, the speaker or presenter has lost the attention of the viewer.

And the expert suggests you would fix this chart by making a scatter plot of the new minimum wage at the time it went into effect vs. the date of that occurrence and then adding a linear regression to emphasize the increase. Use the same for decreases in buying power over time. That would more effectively dramatize the stark difference between the two, which is the message of this chart.

Tables

The major point is that this chart is not about a table. Plus, switching to a table may not have enhanced this chart at all to accomplish its purpose. If the purpose is to convince experts, data shown as a line chart makes sense, especially to demonstrate the sharp trends. For the general public, this information is better served as a simple set of numbers showing an increase in the amount for the minimum wage but a decrease in its buying power over a thirty-year span. A two-number comparison table or even an infographic might be more effective.

APPENDIX
ANALYSIS OF ADDITIONAL
CASE SLIDES

Analysis of Additional Case Study Slides

In this appendix, we shall undertake the analysis of additional slides from the case study. We have covered two of them in the lab book (slides 2 and 4 from the case study slide set). You can use the four additional examples here to further develop your understanding of how to improve data visual in a business context. To show you the usefulness of the analysis template and the process we will use it as the basis for analysis. You can use the template for yourself with each slide and then test your understanding against the remarks by the expert. Take this an assignment: "If I were given these slides to improve, what would I do along the lines of the six dimensions in the lab book, what would I change?" This way, you are further exercising your newly acquired visualization muscles to create compelling visuals.

The premise for our changes will be that there's a desire to reach and convince a more significant portion of the general population about the benefits of the proposed policy change. As it is, the case study charts were probably created to convince economists and policymakers and other trained people of the proposed policy changes. Although some in the general public could understand the charts, they are perhaps out of the reach of the average citizen. That's where you come in. There is a desire by management to create a new set based on these slides that are more accessible to people who not highly educated. Assume that the new slide set will be designed to be used in a presentation, not as a standalone document. Thus, they are to be a set of props for a presenter rather than a report to be read. Your mission: modify the current slides to fit the new audience and the new purpose.

Using the analysis template let's go over four representative slides in the presentation and create new visuals.

Slide 3 – The Big Dip

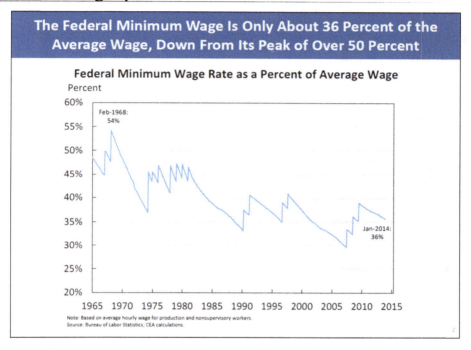

Story Dimension

Visual Story – Is the point of the visual very clear?

Yes, the point of the story is somewhat but not totally clear, especially from the title of the slide. The actual visual does not emphasize the big story. The point of the chart is that there has been a significant drop in minimum-wage as a percentage of average wage from the '60s until the current time. And that story seems to be lost. Yes, there's a peak in 1968 and a low point in 2015, but that significant drop, from 54% to 36%, is not emphasized. That's what the story is, and we are going to convince the general public of that point.

Visual Props – Has the visual has been simplified and focused?

No, this visual is still very much for technical folks. It really won't reach the general public the way it is. The drop from 1968 to 2015 has to be highlighted even more to be effective with a general audience when making a presentation, and when each slide is up on the screen only a few minutes.

Storytellers – Are past masters and the basic charts that they pioneered emulated?

No, this chart doesn't have any pedigree. It's a time series, of course, in the guise of a line chart which were first used by William Playfair over 200 years ago.

What can be done to improve the visual along this dimension?

The numbers at the peak and at the trough, 54%, and 36% should be more distinguishable. Make them more prominent, make them bolder, remove the words in the annotation, and just put large numbers there. The numbers at the peak and the trough, 54% and 36%, should be more prominent. That's what the story is.

Signs Dimension

Signs – Is the use of signs and symbols appropriate?

Yes, there are improvements that can be made to this chart, but in general, it works well in pointing out the significant drop. The significant it is the trend with a peak in 1968 and a low 2015. And it signifies a drop, a steep drop, that is very disturbing. The minimum wage has dropped almost by half as a percentage of the average wage. So, as a sign this slide works pretty well. There are ways in which we can improve this chart, but in general it works well in pointing out the large drop.

Communication – Is the Signal to Noise ratio high?

It takes a bit of work to extract the meaning of the chart. The title helps and the type of chart, time series line chart, also helps. The disparity in the numbers, which is so striking, takes a lot of work to extract from this chart as it is. So, if you may or may not get the message if you viewed this chart for 3-4 minutes (average time for a slide in a presentation). The signal of the considerable drop in minimum-wage as a percentage of average wage gets lost in the noise of a choppy time-series line, additional words explaining the two percentage numbers, and a very wordy slide title. These are lots of noise sources. It needs work.

Function – Is the chart functionally informational rather than beautiful art?

Yes, we would have to say that this is a functional chart, it has been embellished very little. It is very clear.

What can be done to improve the visual along this dimension?

To improve this chart, we have to get our message across more clearly. Do not make the viewer work so hard to extract the story of the considerable drop in the minimum wage.

Purpose Dimension

Need – Does the chart fulfill organizational information needs?

The slide is as it helps economists and policymakers, not so much the general public. So, to get the story out to the ordinary citizen, it will need to be redone. So, whereas it does fulfill your organizational information need, it is not appropriate as a communication vehicle for the new consumer: the public.

Audience – Does the chart allow for audience biases, needs, and journeys?

As it is, no, it will not fulfill the needs of anyone in the new audience, the public. They need the information to know what policies to support and what candidates to vote for in elections. This chart will need to be redone to assist with that.

Frame – Does the visual answer a well-framed analytical question?

Yes, the chart does answer a well-framed analytical question: "what has been the change in the minimum wage as a percentage of the average wage in the last 50 years?"

What can be done to improve the visual along this dimension?

Make it clearer the drop has been dramatic. Perhaps by adding a trend line. Perhaps that making the two extremes the 54% in the 36% Eagles more striking. Otherwise it's pretty good.

Perception Dimension

Seeing – Does the eye of the viewer focus on the most important point being made?

No, the eye doesn't know where to focus when you first view the chart. It probably wanders to the peak on the left-hand side, the 54%. And it may wander down the curve to the low point, the 36%. But there's no real focus to guide the eye to the critical parts of the chart. Because of the boldness and placement, the title of the graph becomes the principal focus of the first look at the chart. That's not an appropriate focal point.

Mind – Have the principles of the Gestalt psychology of perception been thoughtfully employed?

All the slides in the set have the problem of a dark outline enclosing the chart area, and we know from Gestalt that it is probably not needed, or at least should be deemphasized by reducing its voice or removing it entirely.

Quality – Does the visual inform the viewer and dispel his ignorance?

Are we better informed after seeing the slide about this particular point? Unless changes are made to emphasize the importance of the drop from 54% to 36%, we will still be very much in the dark. So, to improve the quality of this chart, we must make it more meaningful, more memorable. It is an excellent point to be raised; thus, if it is successful in presenting it then, yes, we have achieved a quality purpose. But it needs more work so that you can dispel the ignorance of the public on this point.

What can be done to improve the visual along this dimension?

Reduce some of the visual clutter, lower the voice of the outline of the chart, or maybe remove it altogether, lower the font and voice (remove the bolding) of the graph subtitle. Increase the font, change the color, make it bolder, and remove the comments above the 54% and 36% labels. That will make the story very clear.

Method Dimension

Color – Is color used judiciously and sparsely?

The slide follows the color scheme of all the slides in this set, and that is commendable. We should not change any of that. You might want to add some red to continue with the red white and blue color scheme, perhaps making the percentage numbers red. That will make them stand out. And we can use color more effectively.

Chart junk – Is the visual is clear of unnecessary visual elements, not leading to a clear point being made?

The text in the labels accompanying the 54% and 36% numbers is probably chart junk. The fact that we have left in all of the jagged changes in the time series line chart is also considered chart junk. One way to improve on this is to lower the voice of the jagged line, and add a trend line of a different color, perhaps more significant and bolder to connect the 54% of the 36% and one visual sweep. Probably the access title labeled "percent" is chart junk since the numbers on the axis already have the percentage symbol. Use one or the other, but not both. Consider reducing the number of major axis subdivisions from one every 10% to one every 20% and see if that reduces eye clutter further.

Title – Does the title of the chart convey the point being made with the chart?

First, it is good that the chart has a clear title along the lines of what the McKenzie method expects us to do. The chart title is adequate. It could potentially be made more concise - a little more wordsmithing to make it briefer.

What can be done to improve the visual along this dimension?

Make the title shorter and more to the point. Clean up some of the chart junk outlined earlier. Add a bold red trend line to emphasize the drop. Reduce the voice of the jagged data line. Remove the extra words above 54% and 36%. It's probably not necessary to have a link to the source of the data as a footer for a chart that will be used with the general public

Charts Dimension

Right Chart – Does the type of chart being used match the level of judgment required?

Yes, this is probably the right chart type for the level of decision that needs to be made. So, from the Cleveland and McGill scale point of view, this is perhaps the appropriate chart type. The viewer will have to make a decision that the minimum wage as a percentage of the average wage dropped that a great deal over that period of time. And they can judge easily from this type of chart.

Selection – Does the chart type used match the business question being answered?

Yes, the chart type, a line chart for the time series data, is appropriate and matches the business question being answered: "what has been the trend in the last 50 years for the minimum wage as a percentage of the average wage in America?"

Tables – Are referenceable visuals (tables) readable with appropriate conditional formatting and thumbnail graphs used for emphasis?

There's no table here, so no need to do any further analysis on this point. The data does yield to a graph rather than a table, so using a chart was appropriate in this case.

What can be done to improve the visual along this dimension?

Not many changes needed here. The right chart was used, and it helps the viewer make the right business decision.

Slide 4 – The Benefit to Millions

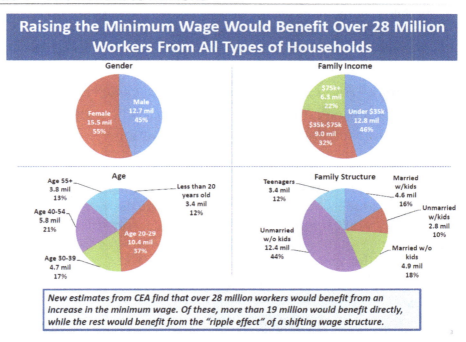

Raising the Minimum Wage Would Benefit Over 28 Million Workers From All Types of Households

New estimates from CEA find that over 28 million workers would benefit from an increase in the minimum wage. Of these, more than 19 million would benefit directly, while the rest would benefit from the "ripple effect" of a shifting wage structure.

Story Dimension

Visual Story – Is the point of the visual very clear?

The point of the story is not very clear, especially connecting the title of the slide to the pie charts. The actual visual itself does match not the banner headline in the title. The point of the chart that is that a significant number of people, namely 28 million, would greatly benefit from an increase the minimum wage. But the mismatch here is between the word "households" and the demographic data that is displayed in the pie charts. The pie charts are not about households but that they represent the demographic of the households that are benefiting from the increase. So perhaps a better title to the slide would fit what is trying to be shown here. The story is that there is great diversity in the gender, age, income and family structure are the demographic breakdown of the 28 million beneficiaries of the increase in minimum wage. The story here is the beneficiaries comprise a wide spectrum of people, not just a narrow element but people from a wide variety of age gender income and family structure spectrums. It's a complex picture. It's a story worth telling but it probably needs a better format for telling it. Or at least a better title. More on this later.

Visual Props – Has the visual has been simplified and focused?

No, this visual it's still not telling a very focused story. It will probably take a storyteller using the current slide as a prop quite a while to explain the meaning of each of the four pie charts. It probably needs a better title. Something like 28 million minimum-wage workers represent a very diverse group of people. This might salvage the slide. The story seems to be about diversity and the title should match. It really won't reach the general public the way it is. They may get something out of it but to get a fuller picture some work needs to be done on this slide.

Storytellers – Are past masters and the basic charts that they pioneered emulated?

Yes, this chart does build on the pedigree of pie charts: William Playfair and Florence Nightingale. And this is an appropriate use of this chart form.

What can be done to improve the visual along this dimension?

Probably write a better title that ties the demographic characteristics to the 28 million beneficiaries of an increase in minimum wage to demonstrate the wide diversity and inclusion represented by the data.

Signs Dimension

Signs – Is the use of signs and symbols appropriate?

Somewhat. The chart does show a breakdown of the composition of the whole of the 28 million by age, by gender, by family income and by type of household. It does give us the demographic breakdown in each of these dimensions, but it doesn't tie into the concept that we have diversity here and that we're serving a lot of different kinds of workers and people and families by increasing the minimum wage. So, the contributions to a whole of the different demographic characteristics represented by the 28 million is a great signifier of the significance of the diversity. But it still does not make it a great sign. The tie between diversity and demographics is tenuous and needs to be strengthened

Communication – Is the Signal to Noise ratio high?

It takes a lot of work to extract the meaning of the chart. The title does not helps let us know that we're going to be shown the diversity by looking at the contribution of each category to the whole. The type of chart, pie, set us up to expect some kind of statement about contributions to the hole. With this title that point is not very clear. It takes a lot of work to extract that fact from this chart as it is. So, if you were in the audience you may or may not get the message. The signal of the diversity in the minimum-wage 28 million recipients gets lost in the noise of a title does not connect. It needs work.

Function – Is the chart functionally informational rather than beautiful art?

Yes, we would have to say that this is a functional chart, it has been embellished very little. The visual part is very clear.

What can be done to improve the visual along this dimension?

To improve this chart, we have to get our message across more clearly. Do not make the viewer work so hard to extract the story of the considerable diversity in the group of minimum-wage workers.

Purpose Dimension

Need – Does the chart fulfill organizational information needs?

The slide is as it helps economists and policymakers, not so much the general public. To get the story of diversity among minimum-wage recipients out to the ordinary citizen will probably need tweaking of the title to work better. So, whereas it does fulfill an organizational information need, it is not appropriate as a communication vehicle get the word to the new consumer: the public.

Audience – Does the chart allow for audience biases, needs, and journeys?

As it is, no, it will not fulfill the needs of the new audience, the general public. They need the information to know what policies to support and what candidates to vote for in elections. This chart will need to be retitled to assist with that.

Frame – Does the visual answer a well-framed analytical question?

Yes, the chart does answer a well-framed analytical question: "is there demographic diversity among the 28 million minimum wage workers?"

What can be done to improve the visual along this dimension?

Make it clearer that the point here is the wide diversity among many demographic characteristics of the 28 million minimum wage beneficiaries.

Perception Dimension

Seeing – Does the eye of the viewer focus on the most important point being made?

No, the eye doesn't know where to focus when you first view the chart. It probably wanders to the title first, and then the brain makes a decision of what seems to be important by what it reads (probably not a good idea, we should be focusing on a picture right away when we see the chart to help us make a quick decision on that.) And then it wanders among the four pie charts, returns to the title, goes to the pie charts to wander some more. There's also visual clutter by the box at the bottom which does distract the eye and probably will not be needed for a general public slide. As it is there is lots of visual noise with no central focus.

Mind – Have the principles of the Gestalt psychology of perception been thoughtfully employed?

employed in the visual?

No major gestalt principles of perception transgressed here. But there is no thoughtful use of them either.

Quality – Does the visual inform the viewer and dispel his ignorance?

Are we better informed after seeing the slide about this particular point? Unless changes are made to tie the four charts to the idea of diversity of the 28 million workers the audience will probably miss the point. So, to improve the quality of this chart, we must make it more meaningful, more memorable, tie it to the point of the diversity of this worker class. It is an excellent point to be raised; thus, if we are successful in presenting it then, yes, we have achieved a quality in our chart. But it needs more work so that you can dispel the ignorance that the public brings to this point.

What can be done to improve the visual along this dimension?

Reduce some of the visual clutter. Tie the title to the charts but making it clear that the slide is about the wonderful diversity of this group of workers. Probably retitling the slide. That will make it very clear what the story is.

Method Dimension

Color – Is color used judiciously and sparsely?

The slide follows the color scheme of all the slides, for the most part. What makes it a little difficult is the introduction of these additional colors of greens the purples in the pie charts that will make it hard for the brain to decode. And then they don't show up anywhere else in the slide set. It would be good to find another color scheme for the pie charts that have more than two segments. One that ties with the prevailing color scheme of red white and blue perhaps shades of red or shades of blue, for example.

Chart junk – Is the visual is clear of unnecessary visual elements, not leading to a clear point being made?

The most obvious eye clutter is the annotation box at the bottom of the chart. Maybe it works for the slide when it was used to inform economists and technical personnel, but it's probably not needed for the set of slides meant for the general public.

Title – Does the title of the chart convey the point being made with the chart?

And now we come to the nub our problem: the title. Clearly this chart could use a better title, one that emphasizes diversity. Also, the pie charts use two different types of labeling. Some segments have outside labels with leader lines, others have the segment titles embedded in the pie section. As a matter of form you should have it one way or the other. It would look cleaner. I suggest in this case you should label all segments with outside with leader lines.

What can be done to improve the visual along this dimension?

A better a title to tie in diversity would be very useful. Removal of some obvious chart junk, such as the box around the annotation at the bottom of the slide. And making all pie segments labels external with leader lines.

Charts Dimension

Right Chart - Does the type of chart being used match the level of judgment required?

Yes, this is probably the right chart type for the level of decision that needs to be made: "Is there diversity among the 28 million minimum wage workers?" The pie charts clearly show that is so in this case, and the appropriate level of definition was employed. The audience can easily judge the wonderful diversity in this group from these charts.

Selection – Does the chart type used match the business question being answered?

Yes, the chart type, a pie chart, is appropriate and matches the business question being answered. In this case it shows contributions of the various demographic segments to the whole of the 28 million workers.

Tables – Are referenceable visuals (tables) readable with appropriate conditional formatting and thumbnail graphs used for emphasis?

There's no table here, so no need to do any further analysis on this point. The data does yield to a graph rather than a table, so using a chart was appropriate here.

What can be done to improve the visual along this dimension?

Not many changes needed here. The right chart was used, and it helps the viewer make the right business decision.

Slide 6 – The Real Reason for the Fall in Poverty Levels

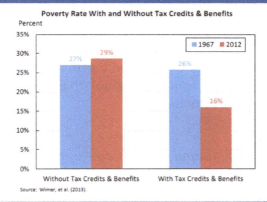

The Poverty Rate Has Fallen Because of Policies Like the Earned Income Tax Credit and Nutrition Assistance, Not Wage Gains

Poverty Rate With and Without Tax Credits & Benefits

The economy has expanded enormously without leading to progress in market-income poverty. Since 1967:
• *Real per capita GDP up 128%*   • *Labor productivity up 142%*   • *Real per capita household wealth up 173%*

One reason for the lack of progress is that the real value of the minimum wage has fallen more than a third from its peak in the late 1960s. Going forward, raising the minimum wage and indexing it to inflation would help to raise wages and reduce poverty.

Story Dimension

Visual Story – Is the point of the visual very clear?

The point of the story is not totally clear. The title of the slide tries to tell the story, but the actual visual itself does not emphasize the big story here. The point of the slide is that, yes there was a drop in poverty levels in the last 50 years but they were other factors besides wage increases for the general population that contributed to the drop. That story seems to be lost here. That's what the story is, and we are going to have to be more convincing here.

Visual Props – Has the visual has been simplified and focused?

Yes, this is a streamlined chart. It is reasonably clean except for the text box at the bottom of the chart. It is probably the wrong chart type but we will discuss that in one of the other dimensions.

Storytellers – Are past masters and the basic charts that they pioneered emulated?

Yes, this chart follows the bar chart format introduced by William Playfair so we can say it does stand on the shoulders of that giant. Very appropriate.

What can be done to improve the visual along this dimension?

As we will see one way to improve the readability of this chart is to change the chart type from a bar graph to a line graph. More on that in one of the other dimensions.

Signs Dimension

Signs – Is the use of signs and symbols appropriate?

The attempt to use a clustered bar graph here for the two series could work as an appropriate significant for the signifier of the drop in poverty levels. But it could be improved. A line graph would be much more appropriate here. The focusing the graph on just the two endpoints 1965 and 2012 to streamline the indication of the drop in poverty levels is very appropriate here. Although the title is much too complex to be understood and a glance, by a simple reading, and needs streamlining.

Communication – Is the Signal to Noise ratio high?

It takes a lot of work to extract the meaning of the chart. Using the wrong chart type make the decoding of the signal: the drop in poverty levels caused by factors other than increases in wages. The other angle, which is not clear from the image, is what is in the title: wages generally went up in the 50-year span but did not affect the drop in poverty level as much as the tax credits and benefit increases. That signal is lost.

Function – Is the chart functionally informational rather than beautiful art?

Yes, we would have to say that this is a functional chart, it has been embellished very little.

What can be done to improve the visual along this dimension?

To improve this chart, we have to get the message across more clearly. The major change we advocate here is the change to a line chart. More on that later.

Purpose Dimension

Need – Does the chart fulfill organizational information needs?

The slide, as is, does not help economists, or policymakers, or the general public. To get the story out to the ordinary citizen, it will need to be redone. The title of the slide is the major fact being presented but the chart as is does not support that conclusion. So, whereas it does fulfill an organizational information need, it is not appropriate as a communication vehicle for the new consumer: the public.

Audience – Does the chart allow for audience biases, needs, and journeys?

As it is, no, it will not fulfill the needs of the new audience, public. They need the information to know what policies to support and what candidates to vote for in elections. This chart will need to be redone to assist with that.

Frame – Does the visual answer a well-framed analytical question?

Yes, the chart does answer a well-framed analytical question: "was the increase in tax credits and benefits a major factor in the drop of the poverty rate to drop in the past 50 years compared to changes in the average wage?"

What can be done to improve the visual along this dimension?

Make it clearer when comparing the beginning and the end of the 50-year period. The type of bar graph being employed does not make it very clear. Which is probably why a switch to a line graph is probably indicated.

Perception Dimension

Seeing – Does the eye of the viewer focus on the most important point being made?

No, the eye doesn't know where to focus when you first view the chart. When you first look at the chart your eye is attracted to the two red bars. Then your eye captures the blue bars at a glance. This does not immediately give you an idea what this chart is about. You then have to go to the title to be able to understand what the chart is telling you. So, your eye being attracted to the red bars, and that is not enough. It's a good place to start. but then your mind wonders: what does it mean? But there's no answer to that question. You have to do a lot of work to connect the facts in the title to the bars on the graph.

Mind – Have the principles of the Gestalt psychology of perception been thoughtfully employed?

employed in the visual?

Probably there's too much chart junk to draw attention away from the main point highlighted by the graphical elements in the center. Besides cleaning up the chart junk certain elements such as the chart sub-title, which is currently bolded, and probably should be deemphasized in favor of the action represented by the bars. Again the outline of the chart is probably not needed. We may not even need any gridlines when we convert to a line graph because we don't want to emphasize precision or accuracy of numbers but we want people to get the main fact of the drop in poverty rate over 50 years due to the tax credits and benefits.

Quality – Does the visual inform the viewer and dispel his ignorance?

Are we better informed after seeing the slide about this particular point? The answer is no, unless changes are made to emphasize the importance of the drop in poverty level over the last 50 years due to tax credits and benefits. So, to improve the quality of this chart, we must make it more meaningful, more memorable. It is an excellent point to be raised; thus, if it is successful in presenting it then, yes, we have achieved a quality purpose. But it needs more work so that you can dispel the ignorance of the public on this point.

What can be done to improve the visual along this dimension?

Reduce some of the visual clutter, lower the voice of the outline of the chart, or maybe remove it altogether, reduce the font and lower the voice (remove the bold font) from the graph subtitle. We probably do not need the grid, as we will discover when we switch to a line graph. That will make it very clear what the story is.

Method Dimension

Color – Is color used judiciously and sparsely?

The slide follows the color scheme of all the slides in this set, and that is commendable. We should not change any of that. When we switch to a line graph, we can make use of the same color scheme: blue for data without tax credits and red for datat with tax credits and benefits, since we want to emphasize the big drop in poverty because of the tax credits and benefits.

Chart junk – Is the visual is clear of unnecessary visual elements, not leading to a clear point being made?

Clearly the box with the comments at the bottom of the chart should be removed for a slide that will be used for the public. That box and its contents do not add to quickly making a point from the title by the use of the image. It should probably go. We might remove the outline of the chart, that's always visually noisy, remove the grid lines, which will make a lot more sense when we go to a line graph. Probably the axis title labeled "percent" is chart junk given that the numbers on the axis already have the percentage symbol. Use one or the other, but not both. Consider reducing the number of major axis subdivisions from one every 10% to one every 20% and see if that reduces eye clutter.

Title – Does the title of the chart convey the point being made with the chart?

First, it is good that the chart has a title along the lines of what the McKenzie method expects us to create. The chart title is probably too long. It could potentially be made more concise - a little more wordsmithing to make it briefer. The connection being made in the title about dropping poverty rate and increase in wage is not born out by the graph itself so one wonders if it should even be there? Unless a connection between these two elements is made in the graph itself, it probably should be removed from the title.

What can be done to improve the visual along this dimension?

Make the title shorter and more to the point. Clean up some of the chart junk outlined earlier. Remove the notation box at the bottom of the chart. Reduce the voice of the title of the graph itself. Remove the percentages above each of the bars. Maybe leaving just won the 16% of the 2012 data point without with tax credits and benefits. It's probably not necessary to have a link to the source of the footer of the chart for a chart that will be used with the general public

Charts Dimension

Right Chart – Does the type of chart being used match the level of judgment required?

As charts go we want an accurate comparison of levels between the years and the conditions so a bar graph or line graph are adequate charts to consider here. From the Cleveland and McGill scale point of view, this is perhaps an appropriate chart. But perhaps not the best chart type, as we discussed next.

Selection – Does the chart type used match the business question being answered?

No, this is probably not the best chart to show this relationship. A much more powerful chart type which would be very effective is to use a line chart. There will be two series, A series colored in red for poverty rate change between 1960 and 2012 with taxt credits and benefits and a series colored blue for the poverty rate change between those two years without. This would be a very clean dramatic difference between the two conditions. It would be a line chart for a time series with two dates, 1960 and 2012. It would definitely highlight the two conditions with and without tax credits and benefits.

Tables – Are referenceable visuals (tables) readable with appropriate conditional formatting and thumbnail graphs used for emphasis?

There's no table here, so no need to do any further analysis on this point. The data does yield to a graph rather than a table, so using a chart was appropriate here.

What can be done to improve the visual along this dimension?

Clearly switching to a line chart with dramatically increase the readability of this graph.

Slide 9 – The Rest of the World

Story Dimension

Visual Story – Is the point of the visual very clear?

Yes, the point of the story very clear especially from the title of the slide. The chart emphasizes the big story here. The point of the chart is that the minimum wage in the US is very far below first world countries, both for the current level in 2016, $7.50, and the proposed rate of $10.10. That's the story and this chart will do a good job convincing the general public of this point.

Visual Props - Has the visual has been simplified and focused?

Yes, this slide could definitely be used as a prop. They may be too many countries, which clutters up the chart a little bit, but in general it does a good job if it's going to be used in a presentation as a prop.

Storytellers – Are past masters and the basic charts that they pioneered emulated?

Yes, this chart follows the bar chart format introduced by William Playfair so we can say it does stand on the shoulders of that giant. Very appropriate. And its formatted as a bar graph and not a column chart which is also a good deployment of this chart type.

What can be done to improve the visual along this dimension?

Not many changes are needed as this is probably a well-executed chart. The title may need a little tweaking.

Signs Dimension

Signs – Is the use of signs and symbols appropriate?

This chart makes the significant, the poor positioning of US minimum-wage with respect to the rest of the world adequately signified by the bar chart. In general, this slide works as a good sign for that purpose.

Communication – Is the Signal to Noise ratio high?

The signal is very strong in this chart. We get the point right away. There's no confusion. The only ambiguity is the red bar seems to have this pink extension and you have to do a little bit of digging to figure out what is the difference between the red bar in the pink bar. With some thinking through the title it finally dawned on you that the red bar ends at the $7.50, 2016 minimum wage, and the pink bar extends it to the proposed $10.10 minimum wage

Function – Is the chart functionally informational rather than beautiful art?

Yes, we would have to say that this is a functional chart, it has been embellished very little. It is very clear.

What can be done to improve the visual along this dimension?

Not much is needed to make this chart more intelligible.

Purpose Dimension

Need – Does the chart fulfill organizational information needs?

The slide, as is, helps both economists, policymakers, and the general public in this case. It will fulfill the informational need of the general public as to where the US minimum wage stands with respect to all the other countries in the world. Clearly the general public will know that after viewing this chart without too much work

Audience – Does the chart allow for audience biases, needs, and journeys?

As it is, yes, it will fulfill the needs of anyone, including the new audience, the public. They need the information to know what policies to support and what candidates to vote for in elections. This chart will not need too much work to do just that.

Frame – Does the visual answer a well-framed analytical question?

Yes, the chart does answer a well-framed analytical question: "where does the United States stand with its level of minimum wage compared to the rest of the world and their minimum wage levels?"

What can be done to improve the visual along this dimension?

Not many changes will be needed to improve this chart.

Perception Dimension

Seeing – Does the eye of the viewer focus on the most important point being made?

Yes, the eye gets drawn immediately to the red bar in the center, which is the United States, and its minimum wage, and makes easy comparisons as the eye roams to the other bars for the levels in other countries. It is an appropriate focal point. There are other distractors that draw attention away from the bars and we will discuss those in the chart junk area.

Mind – Have the principles of the Gestalt psychology of perception been thoughtfully employed?

employed in the visual?

Just like other slides in the set, this particular slide has the same problem of a dark outline enclosing the chart area, and we know from Gestalt that it is probably not needed, or at least should be deemphasized by reducing its voice. We would be well served by removing that outline since Gestalt principles tell us that our mind will enclose the bars if the enclosure is not complete.

Quality – Does the visual inform the viewer and dispel his ignorance?

This is probably one of the higher quality slides in a data set. It is straightforward, easy to read, and quickly informs us of the fact in detail. So yes, the viewer walks away from viewing the slide being better informed, and with their ignorance dispelled. They will know that the US minimum wage is not at one of the highest levels in the world?

What can be done to improve the visual along this dimension?

Just a removal of some small distracting elements that could be distracting to the eye. Otherwise this chart is very usable as is.

Method Dimension

Color – Is color used judiciously and sparsely?

The slide follows the color scheme of all the slides in this set, and that is commendable. We should not change any of that.

Chart junk – Is the visual is clear of unnecessary visual elements, not leading to a clear point being made?

One way to improve on this is to lower the voice of the chart subtitle. And for the General public slide the notation at the bottom referencing the source of the data is probably not needed. When used as a prop that additional charge element is distracting and if an audience member inquiries about it that fact could be delivered by the speaker orally.

Title – Does the title of the chart convey the point being made with the chart?

First, it is good that the chart has a title along the lines of what the McKenzie method expects us to do. The chart title is adequate. It could potentially be made more concise - a little more wordsmithing to make it briefer. Additionally, we can resolve the confusion over the red bar and pink bar extension by adding two direct labels showing the value at the top of those two bars for the current minimum wage in 2016 and the proposed new minimum wage. That will show that neither of those two, $7.50 or $10.10 as minimum wage levels, are adequate compared to the levels in developed economies.

What can be done to improve the visual along this dimension?

Make the title shorter and more to the point. Clean up some of the chart junk outlined earlier. Add a label for the two levels of minimum wage in the US bar.

Charts Dimension

Right Chart – Does the type of chart being used match the level of judgment required?

Yes, this is probably the right chart type for the level of decision that needs to be made. From the Cleveland and McGill scale point of view, this is perhaps the most appropriate chart. The viewer will have to make a decision how the minimum wage do US compares to the rest of the world. And they can judge easily from this chart type.

Selection – Does the chart type used match the business question being answered?

Yes, the chart type, a bar graph (as opposed to a column graph), is appropriate and matches the business question being answered: "how does the US minimum wage compared to the minimum wage in other countries?"

Tables - Are referenceable visuals (tables) readable with appropriate conditional formatting and thumbnail graphs used for emphasis?

There's no table here, so no need to do any further analysis on this point. The data does yield to a graph rather than a table, so using a chart was appropriate here.

What can be done to improve the visual along this dimension?

Not many changes needed here. The right chart was used, and it helps the viewer make the right business decision.

REFERENCES

References

1. Alexander, Christopher. *The timeless way of building*. Vol. 1. Oxford University Press, 1979.

2. Argyris, Chris, and Donald A. Schon. *Theory in practice: Increasing professional effectiveness*. Jossey-Bass, 1974.

3. Bertin, Jacques. "General theory, from semiology of graphics." *The Map Reader: Theories of Mapping Practice and Cartographic Representation* (2011): 8–16.

4. Cairo, Alberto. *The functional art: An introduction to information graphics and visualization*. New Riders, 2012.

5. Cleveland, William S., and Robert McGill. "Graphical perception: The visual decoding of quantitative information on graphical displays of data." *Journal of the Royal Statistical Society, Series A (General)* (1987): 192–229.

6. Cotgreave, Andy. "The 5 Most Influential Data Visualizations of All Time." Tableau, 2013. https://www.tableau.com/learn/webinars/5-most-influential-visualizations-all-time.

7. Few, Stephen. *Now you see it: Simple visualization techniques for quantitative analysis*. Analytics Press, 2009.

8. Kosslyn, Stephen M. *Graph design for the eye and mind*. OUP USA, 2006.

9. Lewis, Richard. *When cultures collide*. Nicholas Brealey Publishing, 2010.

10. Medina, John. *Brain Rules*. Pear Press, 2012.

11. Nussbaumer Knaflic, Cole. "Story Telling with Data: Visualizing Opportunity." Makeovers, September 16, 2015. http://www.storytellingwithdata.com/blog/2015/9/16/visualizing-opportunity.

12. Rosling, Hans. "Hans Rosling shows the best stats you've ever seen, 2006." TED video, February 2006. https://www.ted.com/talks/hans_rosling_the_best_stats_you_ve_ever_seen.

13. Shron, Max. *Thinking with data: How to turn information into insights*. O'Reilly Media, 2014.

14. Thoreau, Henry David. *The writings of Henry David Thoreau.* Vol. V, Houghton-Mifflin, 1884.

15. Tufte, Edward, and P. Graves-Morris. "The visual display of quantitative information; 1983." 2014.

16. Yarbus, Alfred L. "Eye movements during perception of complex objects." *Eye Movements and Vision* (1967): 171–211.

INDEX

www.ingramcontent.com/pod-product-compliance
Lightning Source LLC
Chambersburg PA
CBHW082119070326
40690CB00049B/3951